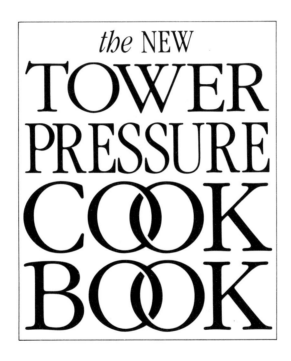

the NEW
TOWER
PRESSURE
COOK
BOOK

Above: Rose Creams (page 90). Right: Marmalade (pages 104, 105). Below: Chinese Lemon Chicken (page 48).

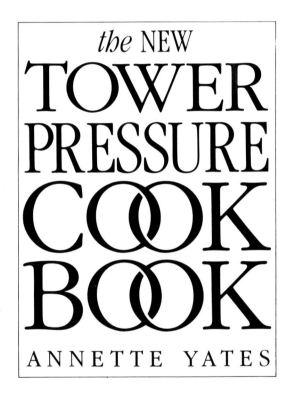

the NEW
TOWER
PRESSURE
COOK
BOOK

ANNETTE YATES

foulsham

LONDON · NEW YORK · TORONTO · SYDNEY

foulsham

Yeovil Road, Slough, Berkshire SL1 4JH

ISBN 0–572–01569–0

Copyright © 1989 W. Foulsham and Co. Ltd

Additional recipes by Hilary Walden

Photography by Mike O'Neill

Home Economist Janet Warren

Printed in Great Britain by Cambus Litho, East Kilbride

Bound by Charles Letts, Dalkeith

CONTENTS

WHY PRESSURE COOKING?

Under-valued and misunderstood, pressure cooking still conjures up images of steamed puddings and limp vegetables. The reality is a lot different – the pressure cooker has the potential to produce the most amazing and exciting meals. This book will lift the lid off pressure cooking and show you how to cook delicious meals suitable for small families or big gatherings; fancy social events or basic economy meals.

The recipes in this book have been selected from round the world: the first section is British since the pressure cooker is ideal for cooking some of our most tasty traditional dishes, the other recipes include Greek, Indian and Spanish among many others. As you experiment you'll find the pressure cooker extraordinarily versatile.

Pressure cooking has many advantages over traditional cooking – first there's speed of cooking: the time required for cooking under pressure is roughly one third that of conventional cooking. And, of course, it is an exceptionally healthy method of preparing food: because a pressure cooker is designed to harness steam, when food is cooked on the trivet vitamins and minerals that would normally be boiled away are retained in the food. Shorter cooking times mean food is less likely to lose colour and also has less time to lose flavour.

The shorter cooking times and the ability to cook several types of food together make the pressure cooker a very economical kitchen appliance. It is also safe and easy to clean – a drop of lemon in boiling water soon cleans any discolouration on the aluminium base.

The recipes in this book have been chosen to show just how versatile your pressure cooker really is. Don't be put off by the myths surrounding this style of cooking, once you start with the simple recipes like Lentil and carrot soup and Quick-baked apples, you'll want to experiment with the more unusual combinations. A complete meal can be prepared in a pressure cooker – meat or fish, vegetables and rice for example, or you can prepare just one delicate and exotic dessert.

Pulses are wonderful cooked under pressure – nutritious and packed with protein they make delicious and colourful dishes. The recipes in the vegetarian section are wonderful combinations of pulses, vegetables, fruits

Opposite: White Tower Speedset Pressure Cooker (Type 1).

and nuts. You can avoid the overnight soaking necessary for conventional cooking: red lentils will cook in 10 minutes at high pressure, borlotti beans take 20 minutes at high pressure and the delicious French flageolet bean (so named because of its resemblance to a flute) cooks in 15 minutes at high pressure. It is important to remember to cook with plenty of liquid – each of the recipes states the exact amount to be used.

Mediterranean dishes are also superb cooked in a pressure cooker. Plaki is a mouthwatering traditional Greek fish casserole easily and quickly prepared. Chicken in almonds and spices is another wonderful Mediterranean dish, a really interesting way to serve chicken with this unusual combination of spices, herbs and nuts. Try the egg and lemon sauce in the recipe for Chicken Avgolomono with pork, or poured over stuffed cabbage.

The most exotic recipes are those in the Far Eastern section. Remarkably easy to prepare and very satisfying to cook, these dishes are spot on for dinner parties and special occasions. A pressure cooker is excellent for experimenting with herbs and spices, remember that the intensive cooking times will increase the strength of the spices. Marinating meat before cooking is an excellent way to tenderize it and also reduces the length of cooking time. Many of the curries will also benefit from standing for an hour or two before being served. Don't forget to add cornflour to any recipe using yogurt, stirred in gently together over a low heat the cornflour will prevent the yogurt curdling.

Whole spices and fresh herbs are well worth buying and do give the edge to these Eastern dishes. Grind or crumble the spices before adding them to the food, and fry to seal in the aromatic flavour. Zaffrani Murgh, chicken with saffron, is one of the most delicious and attractive dishes you can prepare in a pressure cooker. The combination of ginger, coconut, cumin and saffron is enhanced perfectly when all cooked together under pressure. Spanish saffron threads are the best quality, flavour and aroma are delicious and very distinctive (turmeric is not a good substitute!), just pound together the threads and add wine or milk.

Finally don't just reserve your pressure cooker for those delicious steamed puddings – light, airy desserts can be prepared just as easily. Rose creams are the perfect finale to an evening meal and take just 4 minutes to cook.

ALL ABOUT PRESSURE COOKERS

A pressure cooker works by trapping the steam inside the main body of the appliance. An airtight seal prevents the steam escaping and pressure builds up inside. When water is heated under pressure its temperature can rise above 100°C and so food will be cooked more quickly.

Generally, pressure cookers operate at three pressures – 5 lb low pressure for cooking desserts and delicate foods, 10 lb medium pressure best for jams and jellies and 15 lb high pressure suitable for most foods, such as pulses, vegetables, soups and meats.

There are a number of types of pressure cooker on the market, all of which work on the same principle. The first has a pressure weight with an indicator plunger which rises and falls as pressure changes. Rings on the indicator show when a particular pressure has been reached and at this stage the heat must be reduced to maintain the pressure-level. Cooking time begins once the pressure is achieved. Some weights have an audible signal indicating when pressure has been reached. A different type has individual weights for different pressures which need to be fitted firmly at the beginning of cooking.

The pressure can be released in two ways, either by turning off the heat and allowing the pressure to subside slowly or by plunging into cold water to reduce pressure quickly. Slow pressure release is best used for liquid foods like stews and soups which are liable to spurt out of the vent pipe on sudden reduction of pressure. The slow method should also be used for milk puddings which are likely to curdle and for any puddings containing a raising agent.

The most modern models on the market have a unique variable pressure release system allowing the pressure to be released under control without plunging in water.

Most pressure cookers are made of aluminium which is both lightweight and strong. It is ideal for cooking as it spreads heat quickly and evenly over the base area.

Your pressure cooker will come complete with a trivet, which can be removed for soups and stocks, and perforated and unperforated baskets so that different foods can be cooked together.

Remember that to maintain the necessary pressure, a pressure cooker must contain a minimum amount of liquid to produce steam. The longer the cooking time the greater the amount of liquid needed. Amounts of liquid necessary vary from recipe to recipe; as a rule, for cooking times up to 30 minutes use a minimum of $\frac{1}{2}$ pt/300 ml/1$\frac{1}{4}$ cups liquid. Any liquid is appropriate – water can be substituted with beer, stock, cider or wine, but do not use oil as it does not produce steam when heated. (See also pages 112–115.)

9

TRADITIONAL BRITISH COOKERY

The pressure cooker is perfect for cooking traditional British fare, especially casseroles, pot roasts and soups. Pot roasts, such as Beef pot roast and Somerset pork, make a nourishing meal with the vegetables cooked alongside. Make the stock into a tasty gravy to accompany the meat and vegetables. Succulent game dishes, such as Pheasant with apple cream and Pigeon ragout, are cooked in minutes. Your pressure cooker will save you hours of time and effort as versatile soups can be made very quickly too. A good British soup makes a delicious starter or snack, or a filling main meal if served with wholemeal bread.

LENTIL AND CARROT SOUP

INGREDIENTS	IMPERIAL	METRIC	AMERICAN
Butter	1 oz	25 g	2 tbsp
Streaky bacon slices, chopped			
Onion, chopped	1	1	1
Carrots, diced	8 oz	225 g	$\frac{1}{2}$ lb
Lentils	4 oz	100 g	$\frac{1}{4}$ lb
Salt and pepper			
Bouquet garni	1	1	1
Chicken stock	$1\frac{1}{2}$ pt	900 ml	$3\frac{3}{4}$ cups

Heat the butter in the open pressure cooker and sauté the bacon, onion and carrots gently for 4–5 minutes. Stir in the remaining ingredients, bring to pressure and cook for given time. Reduce pressure.

Remove bouquet garni and adjust seasoning if necessary. If a smoother consistency is preferred, liquidize or sieve the soup.

COOKING TIME High/15-lb pressure 10 minutes
Reduce pressure slowly

SERVES 4

Beef Pot Roast (page 20).

TOMATO SOUP

INGREDIENTS	IMPERIAL	METRIC	AMERICAN
Butter	1 oz	25 g	2 tbsp
Celery stick, chopped	1	1	1
Carrot, chopped	1	1	1
Onion, chopped	1	1	1
Streaky bacon slices, chopped	3	3	3
Tomatoes, skinned and sliced	$1\frac{1}{2}$ lb	700 g	$1\frac{1}{2}$ lb
Beef stock	1 pt	550 ml	$2\frac{1}{2}$ cups
Pinch mixed herbs			
Pinch sugar			
Salt and pepper			
Chopped fresh parsley			

Heat the butter in the open pressure cooker and gently sauté the celery, carrot, onion and bacon for 2–3 minutes. Add remaining ingredients, except parsley, bring to pressure and cook for given time. Reduce pressure. Serve garnished with chopped parsley.

COOKING TIME High/15-lb pressure 4 minutes
Reduce pressure slowly

SERVES 4–6

MEAT STOCK

INGREDIENTS	IMPERIAL	METRIC	AMERICAN
Meat bones	2 lb	1 kg	2 lb
Water	2 pt	1.1 l	5 cups
Vegetables such as onions, carrots, celery, swede (or their washed peelings)			
Salt			
Black peppercorns			
Bay leaf	1	1	1

Wash the bones and break them up as small as possible. Place the bones in the open pressure cooker with the water. Bring to the boil slowly, then skim the surface with a metal spoon or a draining spoon. Chop the vegetables and add them with the remaining ingredients, making sure that the cooker is not more than half full. Bring to pressure and cook for given time. Reduce pressure. Strain the stock and leave it to cool before removing surface fat.

COOKING TIME High/15-lb pressure 40 minutes
Reduce pressure slowly

TO FREEZE Divide the stock into suitable quantities, pack and freeze it. Stock 'ice cubes' are useful for adding flavour to gravies etc.

NOTE To make chicken stock, substitute a chicken carcass for the meat bones.

POTATO MINT SOUP

INGREDIENTS	IMPERIAL	METRIC	AMERICAN
Butter	1 oz	25 g	2 tbsp
Potatoes, sliced	1 lb	450 g	1 lb
Water	1 pt	550 ml	$2\frac{1}{2}$ cups
Salt and pepper			
Sprigs of mint	3–4	3–4	3–4
Milk	$\frac{1}{2}$ pt	300 ml	$1\frac{1}{4}$ cups

Heat the butter in the open pressure cooker and sauté the potatoes gently for 2–3 minutes. Stir in the water and season well. Add the mint, bring to pressure and cook for given time. Reduce pressure. Purée or sieve the soup, then return it to the pressure cooker. Stir in the milk, reheat and serve. Garnish with a few sprigs of mint, if liked.

COOKING TIME High/15-lb pressure 5 minutes
Reduce pressure slowly

NOTE Photograph on page 82.

SERVES 4

CREAM OF MUSHROOM SOUP

INGREDIENTS	IMPERIAL	METRIC	AMERICAN
Butter	2 oz	50 g	$\frac{1}{4}$ cup
Mushrooms, sliced	8 oz	225 g	2 cups
Chicken stock	1 pt	550 ml	$2\frac{1}{2}$ cups
Salt and pepper			
Flour	2 tbsp	2 tbsp	2 tbsp
Milk	$\frac{3}{4}$ pt	400 ml	2 cups
Chopped fresh parsley	2 tbsp	2 tbsp	2 tbsp

Melt the butter in the open pressure cooker and gently sauté the mushrooms for a few minutes. Add the stock and season well. Bring to pressure and cook for given time. Reduce pressure.

Mix the flour with a little cold water to form a smooth paste and add this to the soup. Bring to the boil. Stir in the milk and parsley before serving.

COOKING TIME High/15-lb pressure 5 minutes
Reduce pressure slowly

SERVES 4–6

THICK PEA SOUP

INGREDIENTS	IMPERIAL	METRIC	AMERICAN
Dried peas	6 oz	175 g	$1\frac{1}{2}$ cups
Butter	1 oz	25 g	2 tbsp
Medium onion, chopped	1	1	1
Streaky bacon slices, chopped	6	6	6
Chicken stock			
Pinch dried marjoram			
Salt and pepper			
Milk	$\frac{1}{4}$ pt	150 ml	$\frac{2}{3}$ cup

Place the peas in a bowl and cover them with boiling water. Cover with a plate and leave to stand for 1 hour.

Heat the butter in the open pressure cooker and sauté the onion and bacon gently for a few minutes. Strain the peas, reserving the liquid, and add these to the onion mixture. Make up the soaking liquid from the peas to $1\frac{1}{2}$ pt/900 ml/$3\frac{3}{4}$ cups, using chicken stock. Add the stock and marjoram to the pressure cooker, then season well. Bring to pressure and cook for given time. Reduce pressure. Purée the soup and, just before serving, stir in the milk.

COOKING TIME High/15-lb pressure 20 minutes
Reduce pressure slowly

SERVES 4–6

OXTAIL SOUP

INGREDIENTS	IMPERIAL	METRIC	AMERICAN
Cooking oil	1 tbsp	1 tbsp	1 tbsp
Oxtail, jointed	1	1	1
Onions, chopped	2	2	2
Celery sticks, sliced	2	2	2
Carrot, sliced	1	1	1
Beef stock	2 pt	1.1 l	5 cups
Bouquet garni	1	1	1
Salt and pepper			
Butter	1 oz	25 g	2 tbsp
Flour	2–3 tbsp	2–3 tbsp	2–3 tbsp
Lemon juice	1 tsp	1 tsp	1 tsp

Heat the oil in the open pressure cooker and sauté the oxtail and the vegetables gently for 4–5 minutes. Add the stock and bouquet garni and season well. Bring to pressure and cook for given time. Reduce pressure. Strain the soup. Remove the meat from the bones and cut it into small pieces.

Cool the stock (preferably overnight), then skim off the surface fat. In the open pressure cooker or a saucepan, melt the butter. Add the flour and cook gently for a few minutes, stirring well. Slowly add the oxtail stock and bring to the boil, stirring continuously. Add the meat pieces. Adjust seasoning if necessary and add lemon juice just before serving.

COOKING TIME High/15-lb pressure 40 minutes
Reduce pressure slowly

SERVES 4–6

THICK COUNTRY VEGETABLE SOUP

INGREDIENTS	IMPERIAL	METRIC	AMERICAN
Large onions	3	3	3
Large carrots	3	3	3
Large potatoes	3	3	3
Leek	1	1	1
Celery sticks	4	4	4
Butter	1 oz	25 g	2 tbsp
Cooking oil	1 tbsp	1 tbsp	1 tbsp
Can tomatoes	8 oz	225 g	$\frac{1}{2}$ lb
Chicken stock	$1\frac{1}{2}$ pt	900 ml	$3\frac{3}{4}$ cups
Bay leaves	2	2	2
Pinch dried thyme			
Salt and pepper			

Slice all vegetables about $\frac{1}{4}$ inch/0.5 cm thick. Heat the butter and oil in the open pressure cooker and sauté the vegetables gently for about 5 minutes. Add the tomatoes, including their juice, and all remaining ingredients. Stir well, bring to pressure and cook for given time. Reduce pressure. Discard the bay leaves and serve.

COOKING TIME High/15-lb pressure 10 minutes
Reduce pressure slowly

SERVES 6

COCK-A-LEEKIE

INGREDIENTS	IMPERIAL	METRIC	AMERICAN
Chicken joints	3	3	3
Leeks, chopped	1 lb	450 g	1 lb
Chicken stock	$1\frac{1}{2}$ pt	900 ml	$3\frac{3}{4}$ cups
Salt			
Black pepper			

Place the chicken joints and leeks in the pressure cooker and pour in the stock. Season well. Bring to pressure and cook for given time. Reduce pressure.

Remove the chicken joints from the pressure cooker and, when cooled sufficiently, remove the meat from the bones, breaking it into pieces. Return the chicken pieces to the pressure cooker. Adjust seasoning, if necessary, reheat and serve.

COOKING TIME High/15-lb pressure 7 minutes
Reduce pressure slowly

SERVES 4–6

Left: Thick Country Vegetable Soup. Right: Cock-a-Leekie.

STEAK AND KIDNEY PUDDING

INGREDIENTS	IMPERIAL	METRIC	AMERICAN
Filling:			
Stewing steak, cut into cubes	12 oz	350 g	$\frac{3}{4}$ lb
Sheep kidneys, skinned and chopped	4 oz	100 g	$\frac{1}{4}$ lb
Seasoned flour			
Onion, chopped	1	1	1
Salt and pepper			
Beef stock	$\frac{1}{2}$ pt	300 ml	$1\frac{1}{4}$ cups
Suet pastry:			
Self-raising flour, or plain flour sifted with 2 tsp baking powder	8 oz	225 g	2 cups
Pinch salt			
Shredded suet	4 oz	100 g	$\frac{3}{4}$–1 cup
Cold water	$\frac{1}{4}$ pt	150 ml	$\frac{2}{3}$ cup

Coat the steak and the kidney pieces with seasoned flour. Place the meat, onion, seasoning and beef stock into the open pressure cooker. Bring to pressure and cook for given time. Reduce pressure.

Meanwhile, sieve together the flour and salt and stir in the suet. Mix with the cold water to form an elastic dough. Roll two-thirds of the dough into a circle and use it to line a greased 1½-pt/1-1/4-cup basin. Put the steak and kidney in the middle with half of the gravy. Dampen the edges of the dough. Roll remaining dough into a circle and use it to cover the pudding. Press edges together firmly and trim. Cover securely with a piece of foil (make a pleat in the foil to allow the pudding to rise). Pour in 2½ pt/1.5 1/6¼ cups water into the pressure cooker, position the trivet and stand the pudding on top. Close the pressure cooker (do not position the weight) and place it on the heat. When steam begins to escape from the vent in the lid, lower the heat and steam it gently (without the weight) for 15 minutes. Increase the heat, bring to pressure and cook for given time. Reduce pressure.

Serve the pudding from the basin. Heat remaining gravy and serve separately.

COOKING TIME Meat mixture: High/15-lb pressure 15 minutes
Reduce pressure slowly

Pudding: Pre-steaming 15 minutes
Low/5-lb pressure 25 minutes
Reduce pressure slowly

NOTE Pre-steaming is important since this helps give a light result to the suet pastry.

SERVES 4

LAMB HOTPOT

INGREDIENTS	IMPERIAL	METRIC	AMERICAN
Middle neck lamb chops	8	8	8
Cooking oil	2 tbsp	2 tbsp	2 tbsp
Onions, sliced	8 oz	225 g	$\frac{1}{2}$ lb
Carrots, sliced	4 oz	100 g	$\frac{1}{4}$ lb
Potatoes, sliced	1 lb	450 g	1 lb
Salt and pepper			
Stock	$\frac{3}{4}$ pt	400 ml	2 cups

Trim excess fat off the chops. Heat the oil in the open pressure cooker and brown the chops on all sides. Add the onions, carrots and potatoes and cook gently for a further 3–4 minutes. Season well and add the stock. Bring to pressure and cook for given time. Reduce pressure.

If necessary remove some of the surface fat with kitchen paper. Arrange the chops, vegetables and stock in a serving dish, finishing with a layer of potatoes. Brown under a hot grill/broiler before serving.

COOKING TIME High/15-lb pressure 15 minutes
Reduce pressure slowly

SERVES 4

BOILED BEEF AND DUMPLINGS

INGREDIENTS	IMPERIAL	METRIC	AMERICAN
Cooking oil	2 tbsp	2 tbsp	2 tbsp
Brisket, rolled	2½ lb	1.1 kg	2½ lb
Carrots	4	4	4
Small onions	4	4	4
Beef stock	1 pt	550 ml	2½ cups
Bay leaves	2	2	2
Good pinch mace			
Salt and pepper			
Dumplings: Self-raising flour or plain flour sifted with ½ tsp baking powder	4 oz	100 g	1 cup
Shredded or finely chopped suet	2 oz	50 g	½ cup
Small onion, finely chopped	1	1	1
Salt and pepper			
Chopped fresh parsley	1 tbsp	1 tbsp	1 tbsp
Cold water	4 tbsp	4 tbsp	4 tbsp

Heat the oil in the open pressure cooker and brown the beef well on all sides. Arrange the whole carrots and onions around the meat and pour in the beef stock. Add the bay leaves, mace and seasoning. Bring to pressure and cook for given time. Reduce pressure.

Mix together the ingredients for the dumplings, forming the soft dough into eight balls. Return the open pan to the heat and place the dumplings around the meat. Place the lid on the pressure cooker *without the weight or valve* and simmer the dumplings for 10–15 minutes.

Place the meat on a serving dish with the vegetables and the dumplings. Thicken the stock if liked with a little cornflour mixed with cold water and serve it separately.

COOKING TIME High/15-lb pressure 30 minutes
Reduce pressure slowly

SERVES 4–6

OLD FASHIONED BEEF CASSEROLE

INGREDIENTS	IMPERIAL	METRIC	AMERICAN
Lard or dripping	1 oz	25 g	2 tbsp
Stewing steak, cut into cubes	1½ lb	700 g	1½ lb
Onions, sliced	2	2	2
Carrots, sliced	2	2	2
Leeks, sliced	2	2	2
Celery sticks, sliced	2	2	2
Small swede, sliced	½	½	½
Large potatoes, quartered	2	2	2
Beef stock	1 pt	550 ml	2½ cups
Salt and pepper			
Bouquet garni	1	1	1

Heat the lard or dripping in the open pressure cooker and brown the meat for 4–5 minutes. Lift out with a draining spoon. In the same fat sauté the vegetables gently for 3–4 minutes, then stir in the browned meat, beef stock, seasoning and bouquet garni. Bring to pressure and cook for given time. Reduce pressure. Remove bouquet garni.

COOKING TIME High/15-lb pressure 15 minutes
Reduce pressure slowly

SERVES 4–6

FARMHOUSE PÂTÉ

INGREDIENTS	IMPERIAL	METRIC	AMERICAN
Streaky bacon, de-rinded	6 oz	175 g	6 oz
Butter	2 oz	50 g	$\frac{1}{4}$ cup
Lambs' liver, chopped	1 lb	450 g	1 lb
Chickens' livers, chopped	8 oz	225 g	$\frac{1}{2}$ lb
Small onion, chopped	1	1	1
Clove garlic, crushed	1	1	1
Salt			
Black pepper			
Milk	$\frac{1}{4}$ pt	150 ml	$\frac{2}{3}$ cup
Flour	$1\frac{1}{2}$ oz	40 g	$\frac{1}{3}$ cup
Thyme	$\frac{1}{2}$ tsp	$\frac{1}{2}$ tsp	$\frac{1}{2}$ tsp

Stretch the bacon with the blade of a knife, then use it to line a suitable ovenproof container (to fit easily into pressure cooker). Heat the butter in a frying pan and lightly brown the livers, onion and garlic. Season well with salt and black pepper. Purée the liver mixture together with all remaining ingredients. Pour into the prepared container and fold the ends of the bacon on to the pâté. Cover securely with foil. Pour 1 pt/550 ml/2 $\frac{1}{2}$ cups water into the pressure cooker, position the trivet and sit the pâté on top. Bring to pressure and cook for given time. Reduce pressure. Place a saucer/plate/stiff piece of cardboard on the pâté (this should fit neatly inside the container) with a weight on top and allow it to cool before turning it out.

COOKING TIME High/15-lb pressure 25 minutes
Reduce pressure slowly

SERVES 8–10

LEMON CHICKEN

INGREDIENTS	IMPERIAL	METRIC	AMERICAN
Boiling fowl	1	1	1
Juice 1 lemon			
Butter	1 oz	25 g	2 tbsp
Small onions	8 oz	225 g	$\frac{1}{2}$ lb
Carrots	8 oz	225 g	$\frac{1}{2}$ lb
Bay leaves	2	2	2
Black peppercorns	6	6	6
Chicken stock	$\frac{3}{4}$ pt	400 ml	2 cups
Egg	1	1	1
Double/thick cream	4 tbsp	4 tbsp	4 tbsp
Sherry	2 tbsp	2 tbsp	2 tbsp
Blanched almonds	2 oz	50 g	$\frac{1}{2}$ cup

Sprinkle the bird with the lemon juice. Heat the butter in the open pressure cooker and brown the chicken on all sides. Add the whole onions, carrots, bay leaves, peppercorns and chicken stock. Bring to pressure and cook for given time. Reduce pressure.

Place the chicken on a serving dish and arrange the vegetables around. Keep warm. Discard the bay leaves and peppercorns. Beat together the egg and cream and gradually add the hot stock, stirring all the time until thick but smooth. Stir in the sherry and almonds. Pour a little sauce over the chicken and vegetables and serve the remainder separately.

COOKING TIME High/15-lb pressure 10 minutes per 1 lb/450 g
Reduce pressure slowly

SERVES 4–6

BEEF POT ROAST

INGREDIENTS	IMPERIAL	METRIC	AMERICAN
Beef topside/top round	2 lb	1 kg	2 lb
Salt and pepper			
Butter	1 oz	25 g	2 tbsp
Cooking oil	1 tbsp	1 tbsp	1 tbsp
Onion, chopped	1	1	1
Potatoes, halved	4–6	4–6	4–6
Carrots, sliced	4	4	4
Celery sticks, cut up	4	4	4
Beef stock	$\frac{3}{4}$ pt	400 ml	2 cups
Cornflour/cornstarch	2 tbsp	2 tbsp	2 tbsp

Season the topside well with salt and pepper. Heat the butter and oil in the open pressure cooker and brown the beef on all sides. Lift out. In the same fat, sauté the vegetables gently for 2–3 minutes, seasoning well. Lift out with a draining spoon. Pour the stock on to any remaining fat in the pressure cooker, position the trivet and sit the beef on top. Bring to pressure and cook for given time. Reduce pressure. Put the vegetables around the beef, bring to pressure again and cook for given time. Reduce pressure. Arrange on a dish and keep warm.

Mix the cornflour with a little cold water to form a smooth paste and stir it into the stock. Bring to the boil, stirring continuously. Adjust seasoning if necessary. Strain the gravy before serving.

COOKING TIME High/15-lb pressure beef 15 minutes
Reduce pressure quickly
   vegetables added 10 minutes
Reduce pressure slowly

NOTE Photograph on page 10.

SERVES 4–6

SOMERSET PORK

INGREDIENTS	IMPERIAL	METRIC	AMERICAN
Loin pork, rind removed	2 lb	1 kg	2 lb
Salt and pepper			
Cloves	8	8	8
Cooking oil	1 tbsp	1 tbsp	1 tbsp
Large leek, sliced	1	1	1
Large carrots, sliced	2	2	2
Celery sticks, sliced	2	2	2
Dry cider	$\frac{3}{4}$ pt	400 ml	2 cups
Bay leaf	1	1	1
Flour	3 tbsp	3 tbsp	3 tbsp

Season the pork well with salt and pepper. Stick the cloves into the fat side of the meat. Heat the oil in the open pressure cooker and brown the pork on all sides. Remove from pressure cooker. In the same oil sauté the vegetables gently until golden brown, seasoning well. Remove from the pressure cooker. Pour the cider on to any remaining oil and add the bay leaf. Position the trivet and place the pork on top. Bring to pressure and cook for given time. Reduce pressure.

Arrange the vegetables round the pork and bring to pressure again for given time. Reduce pressure. Put the pork and vegetables on a serving dish; keep them warm. Remove the bay leaf. Mix the flour with a little cold water to form a smooth paste and stir it into the sauce. Bring to the boil, stirring continuously. Adjust seasoning if necessary. Serve the sauce separately.

COOKING TIME High/15-lb pressure meat 25 minutes
Reduce pressure quickly
   vegetables added 5 minutes
Reduce pressure slowly

SERVES 4

BACON CASSEROLE WITH DUMPLINGS

INGREDIENTS	IMPERIAL	METRIC	AMERICAN
Bacon collar or slipper joint, cut into cubes	$1\frac{1}{2}$ lb	700 g	$1\frac{1}{2}$ lb
Butter	1 oz	25 g	2 tbsp
Leeks, sliced	1 lb	450 g	1 lb
Chicken stock	$\frac{3}{4}$ pt	400 ml	2 cups
Black pepper			
Dumplings: Self-raising flour or plain flour sifted with 1 tsp baking powder	4 oz	100 g	1 cup
Shredded or finely chopped suet	2 oz	50 g	$\frac{1}{2}$ cup
Small onion, finely chopped	1	1	1
Salt and pepper			
Pinch herbs, such as sage or thyme			
Cold water	4 tbsp	4 tbsp	4 tbsp

Place the bacon cubes in the open pressure cooker and cover them with cold water. Bring slowly to the boil. Discard the liquid and dry the bacon cubes with kitchen paper.

Heat the butter in the open pressure cooker and sauté the leeks and bacon lightly for 3–4 minutes. Add the chicken stock and black pepper. Bring to pressure and cook for given time. Reduce pressure.

Mix together the ingredients for the dumplings, forming the soft dough into eight balls.

Return the open pressure cooker to the heat, bring to the boil and add the dumplings. Place the lid on the pressure cooker *without the weight or valve* and simmer for 10–15 minutes.

COOKING TIME High/15-lb pressure 20 minutes
Reduce pressure slowly

NOTE If a thicker casserole is preferred, stir in some flour mixed to a smooth paste with cold water before adding the dumplings.

SERVES 4

KEDGEREE

INGREDIENTS	IMPERIAL	METRIC	AMERICAN
Long-grain rice	8 oz	225 g	$1-1\frac{1}{4}$ cups
Boiling water, slightly salted	$\frac{3}{4}$ pt	400 ml	2 cups
Smoked haddock fillets	$1\frac{1}{4}$ lb	550 g	$1\frac{1}{4}$ lb
Salt and pepper			
Butter	2 oz	50 g	$\frac{1}{4}$ cup
Hard-boiled eggs, chopped	2	2	2
Single/thin cream	$\frac{1}{4}$ pt	150 ml	$\frac{2}{3}$ cup
Chopped fresh parsley			

Place the rice in an ovenproof bowl and pour on the boiling water. Cover securely with foil. Pour $\frac{1}{2}$ pt/300 ml/$1\frac{1}{4}$ cups water into the pressure cooker and position the trivet. Stand the bowl of rice on the trivet and arrange the seasoned haddock fillets around. Bring to pressure and cook for given time. Reduce pressure.

Remove the bowl of rice, haddock, trivet and water, and wipe the inside of the pressure cooker with kitchen paper. Fluff up the rice with a fork to separate the grains and flake the haddock.

Heat the butter in the open pressure cooker and stir in the rice, fish, chopped hard-boiled eggs and cream. Heat through gently and adjust seasoning if necessary. Serve sprinkled with chopped parsley.

COOKING TIME High/15-lb pressure 5 minutes
Reduce pressure quickly

SERVES 4

BEEF IN BROWN ALE WITH CHEESY TOPPING

INGREDIENTS	IMPERIAL	METRIC	AMERICAN
Lard	2 oz	50 g	$\frac{1}{4}$ cup
Chuck steak, cubed	$1\frac{1}{4}$ lb	550 g	$1\frac{1}{4}$ lb
Onions, sliced	8 oz	225 g	$\frac{1}{2}$ lb
Mushrooms, sliced	4 oz	100 g	1 cup
Brown ale	$\frac{1}{2}$ pt	300 ml	$1\frac{1}{4}$ cups
Beef stock	$\frac{1}{4}$ pt	150 ml	$\frac{2}{3}$ cup
Made mustard	1 tsp	1 tsp	1 tsp
Sugar	2 tsp	2 tsp	2 tsp
Salt and pepper			
Flour	2 tbsp	2 tbsp	2 tbsp
Topping: Small French loaf	1	1	1
Made mustard			
Butter	3 oz	75 g	6 tbsp
Cheese, finely grated	4 oz	100 g	1 cup

Heat the lard in the open pressure cooker and brown the meat lightly. Lift it out with a draining spoon. In the same lard, sauté the onions and mushrooms for 2–3 minutes. Replace meat. Add brown ale, beef stock, mustard and sugar, and season well with salt and pepper. Bring to pressure and cook for given time. Reduce pressure.

Mix the flour with a little cold water to form a smooth paste and stir it into beef mixture. Bring to the boil, stirring well. Arrange meat mixture in an ovenproof serving dish.

Cut the bread into thick slices and spread one side of each slice with mustard. Cream the butter, beat in the cheese and season to taste. Spread the cheese mixture thickly on opposite side of each slice of bread. Then place the bread, cheese side upwards, on top of the beef. Brown under hot grill until the topping is crisp and golden.

COOKING TIME High/15-lb pressure 20 minutes
Reduce pressure slowly

SERVES 4

PIGEON RAGOUT

INGREDIENTS	IMPERIAL	METRIC	AMERICAN
Butter	2 oz	50 g	$\frac{1}{4}$ cup
Small pigeons	4	4	4
Streaky bacon slices, chopped	4	4	4
Tomatoes, skinned and sliced	4	4	4
Beef stock	$\frac{3}{4}$ pt	400 ml	2 cups
Red wine	4 tbsp	4 tbsp	4 tbsp
Salt and pepper			
Flour	1 oz	25 g	$\frac{1}{4}$ cup

Heat the butter in the open pressure cooker and lightly brown the pigeons on all sides. Remove from pressure cooker. In the same butter, sauté the bacon gently for about 2 minutes, then stir in the tomatoes, beef stock and red wine. Return the pigeons to the pressure cooker and season with salt and pepper. Bring to pressure and cook for given time. Reduce pressure.

Using a draining spoon, lift the pigeons on to a serving dish. Mix the flour with a little cold water to form a smooth paste. Add it to the sauce and bring to the boil, stirring continuously. Adjust seasoning if necessary. Pour the sauce over and around the pigeons and serve with pieces of fried bread and watercress, if liked.

COOKING TIME High/15-lb pressure 10 minutes
Reduce pressure slowly

SERVES 4

Above: Beef in Brown Ale with Cheesy Topping. Below: Pigeon Ragout.

CELERY IN TOMATO

INGREDIENTS	IMPERIAL	METRIC	AMERICAN
Butter	1 oz	25 g	2 tbsp
Clove garlic, crushed	1	1	1
Large head celery, cut into sticks	1	1	1
Can tomatoes	8 oz	225 g	$\frac{1}{2}$ lb
Pinch mixed herbs			
Chicken stock	$\frac{1}{4}$ pt	150 ml	$\frac{2}{3}$ cup
Salt and pepper			
Flour	1–2 tbsp	1–2 tbsp	1–2 tbsp

Heat the butter in the open pressure cooker and sauté the garlic and celery gently for 1–2 minutes. Pour the tomatoes and their juices over the celery and add the mixed herbs, chicken stock and seasoning. Stir well, bring to pressure and cook for given time. Reduce pressure.

Mix the flour with a little cold water to form a smooth paste and stir it into the sauce. Bring to the boil, stirring.

COOKING TIME High/15-lb pressure 4 minutes
Reduce pressure quickly

SERVES 4

MUSTARD RABBIT

INGREDIENTS	IMPERIAL	METRIC	AMERICAN
Butter	2 oz	50 g	$\frac{1}{4}$ cup
Rabbit joints	$1\frac{1}{2}$ lb	700 g	$1\frac{1}{2}$ lb
Streaky bacon, chopped	8 oz	225 g	$\frac{1}{2}$ lb
Large onions, chopped	3	3	3
Chicken stock	1 pt	550 ml	$2\frac{1}{2}$ cups
Salt and pepper			
Bouquet garni	1	1	1
French mustard	1 tbsp	1 tbsp	1 tbsp
Flour	3 tbsp	3 tbsp	3 tbsp

Heat the butter in the open pressure cooker and lightly brown the rabbit joints. Lift them out. In the same butter, sauté the bacon and onions for 2–3 minutes. Replace the rabbit and add the chicken stock, seasoning, bouquet garni and mustard. Bring to pressure and cook for given time. Reduce pressure. Mix the flour with a little cold water to form a smooth paste and stir it into the casserole. Bring to the boil, stirring well.

COOKING TIME High/15-lb pressure 15 minutes
Reduce pressure slowly

SERVES 4

PHEASANT WITH APPLE CREAM

INGREDIENTS	IMPERIAL	METRIC	AMERICAN
Small pheasants	2	2	2
Seasoned flour			
Butter	2 oz	50 g	$\frac{1}{4}$ cup
Cooking apples, peeled, cored and sliced	4	4	4
Beef stock	$\frac{1}{2}$ pt	300 ml	$1\frac{1}{4}$ cups
Double/thick cream	$\frac{1}{4}$ pt	150 ml	$\frac{2}{3}$ cup
Watercress, to garnish			

Coat the pheasants with seasoned flour. Heat the butter in the open pressure cooker and brown the pheasant on all sides. Lift them out. In the same butter, sauté the apples gently for 2–3 minutes. Replace the pheasants and pour the beef stock around them. Bring to pressure and cook for given time. Reduce pressure.

Place the pheasants on a serving dish and keep them warm. Purée or mash the apple mixture and adjust the seasoning if necessary. Stir in the cream. Garnish the pheasants with watercress and serve the sauce separately.

COOKING TIME High/15-lb pressure 8 minutes
Reduce pressure quickly

SERVES 4

DUCKLING CASSEROLE

INGREDIENTS	IMPERIAL	METRIC	AMERICAN
Butter	1 oz	25 g	2 tbsp
Duckling joints	4	4	4
Onions, sliced	2	2	2
Carrots, sliced	2	2	2
Chicken stock	$\frac{3}{4}$ pt	400 ml	2 cups
Bay leaf	1	1	1
Chopped fresh parsley	2 tsp	2 tsp	2 tsp
Dried oregano	$\frac{1}{2}$ tsp	$\frac{1}{2}$ tsp	$\frac{1}{2}$ tsp
Salt and pepper			
Cornflour/cornstarch	3 tbsp	3 tbsp	3 tbsp

Heat the butter in the open pressure cooker and brown the duckling joints well on all sides. Remove the duckling from the pressure cooker. In the same butter, sauté the onions and carrots gently for about 2 minutes. Add the browned duckling joints, chicken stock, bay leaf, parsley and oregano. Season well, bring to pressure and cook for given time. Reduce pressure. Discard the bay leaf.

Using kitchen paper or a metal spoon, remove excess fat from the surface of the sauce. Mix the cornflour with a little cold water to form a smooth paste. Add it to the pressure cooker and bring to the boil, stirring continuously.

COOKING TIME High/15-lb pressure 12 minutes
Reduce pressure slowly

SERVES 4

STUFFED CABBAGE

INGREDIENTS	IMPERIAL	METRIC	AMERICAN
Butter	1 oz	25 g	2 tbsp
Minced/ground beef	1 lb	450 g	1 lb
Small onion, chopped	1	1	1
Clove garlic, crushed	1	1	1
Cooked long-grain rice	1 oz	25 g	2–3 tbsp
Good pinch mixed herbs			
Good pinch mixed spice			
Salt and pepper			
Large cabbage leaves	12	12	12
Beef stock	$\frac{1}{2}$ pt	300 ml	$1\frac{1}{4}$ cups
Can condensed tomato soup	$10\frac{1}{2}$ oz	298 g	medium

Heat the butter in a frying pan and brown the minced beef for 4–5 minutes. Stir in the onion and garlic and cook gently for a further few minutes. Stir in the rice, herbs, spice and seasoning.

Blanch the cabbage leaves in boiling water for 2 minutes. Dry well with kitchen paper. Place some filling in the centre of each leaf and roll up the leaf, tucking in the ends to form neat parcels. Arrange the cabbage rolls in the pressure cooker (without the trivet) and pour the beef stock around the rolls. Bring to pressure and cook for given time. Reduce pressure.

Lift the cabbage on to a warm serving dish. Carefully stir the condensed soup into the stock and reheat. Pour some sauce over and around the cabbage and serve the rest separately.

COOKING TIME High/15-lb pressure 15 minutes
Reduce pressure quickly

SERVES 6

MEDITERRANEAN COOKERY

Sunny Mediterranean recipes, reminding us of holidays we enjoyed, can be prepared with ease in your pressure cooker. Start a meal with delicious Greek Hummous, French Vichyssoise or Italian Minestrone soup. Main courses, such as Beef Bourguignon, Chicken avgolomono or Pork with wine and coriander, are prepared in a fraction of the normal cooking time; making them ideal entertaining dishes to impress family and friends alike.

VICHYSSOISE

INGREDIENTS	IMPERIAL	METRIC	AMERICAN
Butter	3 oz	75 g	6 tbsp
Leeks, sliced	6	6	6
Onions, sliced	2	2	2
Potatoes, thinly sliced	2	2	2
Salt and pepper			
Chicken stock	$1\frac{3}{4}$ pt	1 l	$4\frac{1}{4}$ cups
Sprigs of parsley	2–3	2–3	2–3
Single/thin cream	$\frac{1}{2}$ pt	300 ml	$1\frac{1}{4}$ cups
Chopped chives, to garnish			

Heat the butter in the open pressure cooker and sauté the vegetables for 2–3 minutes without browning them. Season and add the chicken stock and parsley sprigs. Bring to pressure and cook for given time. Reduce pressure.

Remove the parsley sprigs. Purée or sieve the soup and cool. Stir the cream into the chilled soup just before serving, garnished with chopped chives.

COOKING TIME High/15-lb pressure 6 minutes
Reduce pressure slowly

NOTE This soup may also be served hot with the cream stirred in just before serving.

SERVES 6

Hummous (page 28).

PORK AND BACON PÂTÉ

INGREDIENTS	IMPERIAL	METRIC	AMERICAN
Streaky bacon	8 oz	225 g	$\frac{1}{2}$ lb
Pork, minced/ground	1 lb	450 g	1 lb
Small onion, minced/ground	1	1	1
Fresh white breadcrumbs	6 oz	175 g	3 cups
Mushrooms, finely chopped	2 oz	50 g	$\frac{1}{2}$ cup
Salt	2 tsp	2 tsp	2 tsp
Black pepper	1 tsp	1 tsp	1 tsp
Ground mace	2 tsp	2 tsp	2 tsp
Eggs, beaten	2	2	2

Remove the rind from the bacon and stretch the bacon with the blade of a knife. Use it to line a suitable ovenproof container (about 6 inches/15 cm diameter). Mix together the remaining ingredients and press them firmly into the prepared container, folding the ends of the bacon on to the pâté. Cover securely with foil. Pour 1 pt/550 ml/$2\frac{1}{2}$ cups water into the pressure cooker and position the trivet. Stand the pâté on top. Bring to pressure and cook for given time. Reduce pressure.

Put a plate on top of the pâté and weight it down. Cool like this before turning out. Serve with toast.

COOKING TIME High/15-lb pressure 25 minutes
Reduce pressure slowly

SERVES 8–10

HUMMOUS

Ingredients	Imperial	Metric	American
Chick peas	4 oz	100 g	generous $\frac{1}{2}$ cup
Tahina*	3 tbsp	3 tbsp	3 tbsp
Cloves garlic, chopped	2	2	2
Juice of 1 lemon			
Olive oil	2 tbsp	2 tbsp	2 tbsp
Salt and pepper			
Olive oil, paprika pepper, finely chopped fresh mint or parsley and pitta bread, to serve			

Pour boiling water over the chick peas and leave to soak for 1 hour. Drain the chick peas and place in the pressure cooker with 1 pt/550 ml/2 $\frac{1}{2}$ cups water. Bring to the boil in the open pressure cooker, remove the scum from the surface, adjust the heat so the contents just boil but do not rise in the cooker. Bring to pressure over the same heat and cook for given time. Reduce pressure.

Drain the chick peas, reserving 4 fl oz/100 ml/$\frac{1}{2}$ cup of the cooking liquor. Purée the chick peas, reserved cooking liquor, tahina, garlic, lemon juice and olive oil. Season to taste and spoon into a bowl. Trickle a circle of oil over the surface and sprinkle paprika pepper and chopped mint or parsley. Serve with pitta bread.

Cooking Time High/15-lb pressure 20 minutes
Reduce pressure slowly

Note Tahina, also spelt tahini, is a ground sesame seed paste. It is available in jars from ethnic shops, delicatessens and good supermarkets. Photograph on page 26.

SERVES 4–6

MINESTRONE

Ingredients	Imperial	Metric	American
Butter	1 oz	25 g	2 tbsp
Streaky bacon slices, chopped	3	3	3
Onion, chopped	1	1	1
Clove garlic, crushed	1	1	1
Leek, sliced	1	1	1
Carrot	1	1	1
Celery stick, sliced	1	1	1
Cabbage, shredded	$\frac{1}{4}$	$\frac{1}{4}$	$\frac{1}{4}$
Runner beans or green beans, sliced	4	4	4
Peas, shelled	1 oz	25 g	$\frac{1}{4}$ cup
Tomato purée/paste	2 tbsp	2 tbsp	2 tbsp
Salt and pepper			
Chicken stock or water	2 pt	1.1 l	5 cups
Macaroni, spaghetti or pasta shapes	1 oz	25 g	$\frac{1}{4}$ cup

Heat the butter in the open pressure cooker and sauté the bacon and vegetables gently for 2–3 minutes. Add the remaining ingredients, bring to pressure and cook for given time. Reduce pressure. Adjust seasoning if necessary.

Cooking Time High/15-lb pressure 8 minutes
Reduce pressure slowly

Note Vegetables for this soup may be varied according to the season.

SERVES 4–6

PAPRIKA LAMB CUTLETS

INGREDIENTS	IMPERIAL	METRIC	AMERICAN
Butter	1 oz	25 g	2 tbsp
Lamb cutlets	8	8	8
Onion, chopped	1	1	1
Small green pepper, de-seeded and chopped	1	1	1
Paprika pepper	3 tsp	3 tsp	3 tsp
Chicken stock	$\frac{1}{2}$ pt	300 ml	$1\frac{1}{4}$ cups
Bay leaf	1	1	1
Tomato purée/paste	2 tbsp	2 tbsp	2 tbsp
Sugar	2 tsp	2 tsp	2 tsp
Salt and pepper			
Carrots, quartered	4	4	4
New potatoes	16	16	16
Butter			
Chopped fresh parsley			
Cornflour/cornstarch	2 tbsp	2 tbsp	2 tbsp

Heat the butter in the open pressure cooker and brown the cutlets quickly. Add the onion, green pepper, paprika pepper, chicken stock, bay leaf, tomato purée and sugar. Season to taste. Place the trivet on the cutlets and arrange the carrots and potatoes on top. Season with salt and pepper. Bring to pressure and cook for given time. Reduce pressure. Arrange the vegetables on a serving dish, dot with butter and sprinkle with chopped parsley. Keep warm.

Arrange the cutlets on a serving dish and keep them warm. Mix the cornflour with a little cold water to form a smooth paste and add it to the paprika sauce. Bring to the boil, stirring well.

COOKING TIME High/15-lb pressure 10 minutes
Reduce pressure quickly

SERVES 4

LAMB CUTLETS ITALIAN STYLE

INGREDIENTS	IMPERIAL	METRIC	AMERICAN
Cooking oil	2 tbsp	2 tbsp	2 tbsp
Salt and pepper			
Lamb cutlets	8	8	8
Large onion, chopped	1	1	1
Clove garlic, crushed	1	1	1
Large carrot, chopped	1	1	1
Can tomatoes	14 oz	397 g	1 lb
Dried oregano	1 tsp	1 tsp	1 tsp
Flour	2 tbsp	2 tbsp	2 tbsp

Heat the oil in the open pressure cooker and brown the well seasoned cutlets on each side. Remove from pressure cooker. In the same oil sauté the onion, garlic and carrot for 2–3 minutes. Add the tomatoes (including juice) and oregano. Place the trivet on top of the vegetables and arrange the cutlets on the trivet. Bring to pressure and cook for given time. Reduce pressure.

Transfer the cutlets to a serving dish and keep them warm. Mix the flour with a little cold water to form a smooth paste and stir it into the sauce. Bring to the boil, stirring continuously. Pour the sauce over the cutlets and serve.

COOKING TIME High/15-lb pressure 10 minutes
Reduce pressure quickly

SERVES 4

TAGINE

INGREDIENTS	IMPERIAL	METRIC	AMERICAN
Olive oil	3 tbsp	3 tbsp	3 tbsp
Boneless lean lamb, cut into large pieces	$1\frac{1}{4}$ lb	550 g	$1\frac{1}{4}$ lb
Large onion, finely chopped	1	1	1
Clove garlic, finely crushed	1	1	1
Saffron threads	$\frac{1}{2}$ tsp	$\frac{1}{2}$ tsp	$\frac{1}{2}$ tsp
Ground ginger	$\frac{1}{2}$ tsp	$\frac{1}{2}$ tsp	$\frac{1}{2}$ tsp
Ground cinnamon	1 tsp	1 tsp	1 tsp
Veal stock	$\frac{3}{4}$ pt	425 ml	2 cups
Prunes, stoned/pitted, soaked for 10 minutes in hot water, drained	4 oz	100 g	$\frac{1}{4}$ lb
Dried apricots	4 oz	100 g	$\frac{1}{4}$ lb
Pine nuts	2 oz	50 g	$\frac{1}{2}$ cup
Orange flower water	1 tbsp	1 tbsp	1 tbsp
Black pepper			
Handful of fresh coriander, chopped, to garnish			

Heat about 2 tbsp of the oil in the open pressure cooker and sauté the lamb, stirring occasionally, until a light even brown. Remove with a slotted spoon, place on kitchen paper and keep warm. Add the onion and garlic to the cooker and cook, stirring occasionally, until softened but not coloured. Stir in the saffron, ginger and cinnamon and heat for 2 minutes. Return the meat to the cooker. Stir in the stock, bring to pressure and cook for 10 minutes. Reduce pressure. Add the dried fruits, return to pressure and cook for given time. Meanwhile, fry the pine nuts in the remaining oil.

Reduce pressure. Lift out the meat using a slotted spoon and keep warm. Boil the cooking juices hard until reduced. Add orange flower water and seasoning to taste. Return the meat to the cooker, stirring to coat in the sauce. Scatter the nuts and coriander over.

COOKING TIME High/15-lb pressure lamb 10 minutes
dried fruits added 5 minutes
Reduce pressure slowly

SERVES 4

BEEF BOURGUIGNON

INGREDIENTS	IMPERIAL	METRIC	AMERICAN
Butter	2 oz	50 g	$\frac{1}{4}$ cup
Chuck steak, cubed	$1\frac{3}{4}$ lb	800 g	$1\frac{3}{4}$ lb
Onions, chopped	2	2	2
Clove garlic, crushed	1	1	1
Streaky bacon, chopped	4 oz	100 g	$\frac{1}{4}$ lb
Red wine	$\frac{3}{4}$ pt	425 ml	2 cups
Bouquet garni	1	1	1
Salt and pepper			
Button mushrooms	8 oz	225 g	2 cups
Flour	2–3 tbsp	2–3 tbsp	2–3 tbsp
Chopped fresh parsley, to garnish			

Heat the butter in the open pressure cooker and brown the meat for 3–4 minutes. Lift it out with a draining spoon. In the same butter sauté the onions, garlic and bacon gently until transparent. Return the meat to the pressure cooker and add the red wine, bouquet garni, seasoning and mushrooms. Bring to pressure and cook for given time. Reduce pressure. Remove bouquet garni.

Mix the flour with a little cold water to form a smooth paste and add to the beef. Bring to the boil, stirring well.

COOKING TIME High/15-lb pressure 20 minutes
Reduce pressure slowly

SERVES 4

Above: Tagine. Below: Beef Bourguignon.

BOLOGNESE SAUCE

INGREDIENTS	IMPERIAL	METRIC	AMERICAN
Cooking oil	2 tbsp	2 tbsp	2 tbsp
Large onions, chopped	2	2	2
Clove garlic, crushed	1	1	1
Bacon (streaky), chopped	4 oz	100 g	$\frac{1}{4}$ lb
Minced/ground beef	1 lb	450 g	1 lb
Can tomatoes	14 oz	397 g	1 lb
Beef stock	$\frac{1}{2}$ pt	300 ml	$1\frac{1}{4}$ cups
Salt and pepper			

Heat the oil in the open pressure cooker and sauté the onions, garlic and bacon gently for about 2 minutes. Add the minced beef and cook for a further few minutes until the mince is lightly browned. Add the remaining ingredients, bring to pressure and cook for given time. Reduce pressure.

If necessary, return the open pressure cooker to the heat and cook the sauce for a few minutes to reduce and thicken it. Serve with buttered spaghetti.

COOKING TIME High/15-lb pressure 15 minutes
Reduce pressure slowly

SERVES 4–6

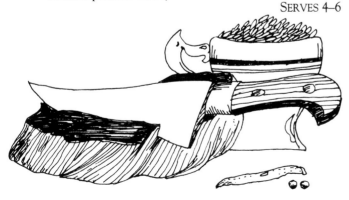

PORK WITH WINE AND CORIANDER

INGREDIENTS	IMPERIAL	METRIC	AMERICAN
Cloves garlic, crushed	2	2	2
Olive oil	3 tbsp	3 tbsp	3 tbsp
Medium or full bodied red wine	$\frac{1}{2}$ pt	300 ml	$1\frac{1}{4}$ cups
Loin of pork, cubed	$1\frac{1}{2}$ lb	700 g	$1\frac{1}{2}$ lb
Coriander seeds, crushed	1 tbsp	1 tbsp	1 tbsp
Large onion, diced	1	1	1
Unsalted butter, diced	$1\frac{1}{2}$ oz	40 g	3 tbsp
Salt and pepper			
Sprigs of coriander or parsley and olives, to garnish			

Mix together the garlic, half of the oil and half of the wine. Put the pork into a wide, shallow, non-metallic dish, pour the wine mixture over, turn the pork in the liquid. Cover and leave in a cool place for 2–3 hours. Drain the liquid from the pork. Heat the remaining oil in the open pressure cooker, add the coriander seeds and cook, stirring occasionally, for 2–3 minutes. Remove, using a slotted spoon, and crush finely. Stir the onion into the cooker and cook, stirring occasionally until softened but not coloured. Remove. Add the pork to the cooker and brown evenly. Add the reserved marinade, remaining wine, coriander and onion. Bring to pressure and cook for given time. Reduce pressure.

Transfer the pork to a warmed dish, using a slotted spoon, and keep warm. Boil the cooking juices in the open cooker until lightly syrupy. Lower the heat and gradually whisk in the butter – do not allow to boil. Taste and adjust the seasoning. Pour over the meat and garnish with coriander or parsley and olives.

COOKING TIME High/15-lb pressure 6 minutes
Reduce pressure quickly

NOTE Photograph on page 38.

SERVES 4

VEAL ROLL WITH HERBS

INGREDIENTS	IMPERIAL	METRIC	AMERICAN
Loin veal, boned	$2\frac{1}{2}$ lb	1.1 kg	$2\frac{1}{2}$ lb
Cooking oil	2 tbsp	2 tbsp	2 tbsp
Pinch each of thyme, basil, cloves and mace			
Juice 1 lemon			
Small potatoes	8	8	8
Small carrots	4	4	4
Small onions	4	4	4
Salt and pepper			
Onion stock/bouillon cube	1	1	1
Water	$\frac{3}{4}$ pt	400 ml	2 cups
Flour	3 tbsp	3 tbsp	3 tbsp

Roll the veal tightly and tie securely with string. Mix together half of the oil with the thyme, basil, cloves, mace and lemon juice. Brush the mixture all over the veal roll. Heat the remaining oil in the open pressure cooker and brown the meat on all sides and both ends. Remove from the pressure cooker. In the same oil, sauté the whole vegetables until lightly browned, seasoning well. Remove from the pressure cooker. Dissolve the stock cube in the water and pour it into the pressure cooker. Place trivet in position with the veal roll on top. Pour any remaining herb/lemon mixture over the veal, bring to pressure and cook for given time. Reduce pressure.

Put the vegetables around the veal and bring to pressure again for given time. Reduce pressure.

Slice the veal and arrange it on a serving dish with the vegetables. Keep warm. Mix the flour with a little cold water to form a smooth paste and stir this into the sauce. Bring to the boil, stirring well. Pour a little over the veal slices and serve the rest separately.

COOKING TIME High/15-lb pressure meat 20 minutes
Reduce pressure quickly
   vegetables added 7 minutes
Reduce pressure slowly

SERVES 4

VEAL AND MUSHROOM CREAM

INGREDIENTS	IMPERIAL	METRIC	AMERICAN
Pie veal, cut into cubes	$1\frac{1}{2}$ lb	700 g	$1\frac{1}{2}$ lb
Seasoned flour			
Butter	2 oz	50 g	$\frac{1}{4}$ cup
Onion, chopped	1	1	1
Clove garlic, crushed (optional)	1	1	1
Pinch dried thyme			
Dry cider	$\frac{1}{2}$ pt	300 ml	$1\frac{1}{4}$ cups
Salt and pepper			
Mushrooms, sliced	8 oz	225 g	2 cups
Single/thin cream	6 fl oz	175 ml	$\frac{3}{4}$ cup
Watercress, to garnish			

Coat the veal with seasoned flour. Heat the butter in the open pressure cooker and lightly brown the veal. Add the onion and garlic and cook for a further minute. Add the thyme, cider and seasoning, then stir in the mushrooms. Bring to pressure and cook for given time. Reduce pressure. Stir in the cream just before serving. Garnish with watercress.

COOKING TIME High/15-lb pressure 12 minutes
Reduce pressure slowly

SERVES 4

PLAKI

INGREDIENTS	IMPERIAL	METRIC	AMERICAN
Olive oil	3 tbsp	3 tbsp	3 tbsp
Onions, sliced	2	2	2
Cloves garlic, crushed	2	2	2
Carrot, sliced	1	1	1
Celery stick, sliced	1	1	1
Red pepper, de-seeded and sliced	1	1	1
Tomatoes, skinned, de-seeded, chopped	1 lb	450 g	1 lb
Tomato purée/paste	2 tsp	2 tsp	2 tsp
Chopped fresh oregano	1–2 tsp	1–2 tsp	1–2 tsp
Halibut, cut into steaks	$1\frac{1}{2}$ lb	700 g	$1\frac{1}{2}$ lb
Medium-bodied dry white wine	$\frac{1}{4}$ pt	150 ml	$\frac{2}{3}$ cup
Fish stock	$\frac{1}{4}$ pt	150 ml	$\frac{2}{3}$ cup
Salt and pepper			
Stoned/pitted black olives and chopped fresh parsley, to garnish			

Heat the oil in the open pressure cooker and sauté the onion, stirring occasionally, until beginning to colour. Add the garlic, carrot, celery and red pepper and cook over a low heat for 2–3 minutes. Add the tomatoes, tomato purée and oregano, place the fish on the vegetables and pour the wine and stock over. Bring to pressure and cook for given time. Reduce pressure.

Transfer the fish to a warmed serving dish and keep warm. Boil the cooking liquid to thicken slightly. Adjust the seasoning and amount of tomato purée and oregano, if necessary, then pour over the fish. Scatter olives and plenty of parsley over.

COOKING TIME High/15-lb pressure $2\frac{1}{2}$ minutes
Reduce pressure quickly

SERVES 4

RATATOUILLE

INGREDIENTS	IMPERIAL	METRIC	AMERICAN
Cooking oil	4 tbsp	4 tbsp	4 tbsp
Onions, chopped	2	2	2
Cloves garlic, crushed	1–2	1–2	1–2
Green peppers, de-seeded and sliced	2	2	2
Tomatoes, skinned and sliced	1 lb	450 g	1 lb
Large aubergine/ eggplant, sliced	1	1	1
Courgettes/zucchini, sliced	4	4	4
Water	$\frac{1}{4}$ pt	150 ml	$\frac{2}{3}$ cup
Tomato purée/paste	2 tbsp	2 tbsp	2 tbsp
Salt and pepper			

Heat the oil in the open pressure cooker and sauté the onions and garlic until transparent. Stir in the remaining ingredients, bring to pressure and cook for given time. Reduce pressure.

COOKING TIME High/15-lb pressure 5 minutes
Reduce pressure quickly

SERVES 4–6

TURKEY MARENGO

INGREDIENTS	IMPERIAL	METRIC	AMERICAN
Turkey joints	4	4	4
Salt and pepper			
Cooking oil	2 tbsp	2 tbsp	2 tbsp
Clove garlic, crushed	1	1	1
Large onion, sliced	1	1	1
Carrots, sliced	2	2	2
Can tomatoes	14 oz	397 g	1 lb
Chicken stock	$\frac{1}{4}$ pt	150 ml	$\frac{2}{3}$ cup
Button mushrooms	4 oz	100 g	1 cup
Bay leaf	1	1	1
Bouquet garni	1	1	1
Flour	2 tbsp	2 tbsp	2 tbsp

Season the turkey joints well with salt and pepper. Heat the oil in the open pressure cooker and brown the turkey joints on all sides. Remove them from the pressure cooker. In the same oil, sauté the garlic, onion and carrots gently for about 2 minutes. Add the browned turkey joints, tomatoes, chicken stock, mushrooms, bay leaf and bouquet garni. Bring to pressure and cook for given time. Reduce pressure. Discard bay leaf and bouquet garni. Mix the flour with a little cold water to form a smooth paste. Stir into the turkey mixture and bring to the boil.

COOKING TIME High/15-lb pressure 10 minutes
Reduce pressure quickly

SERVES 4

CYPRUS CHICKEN

INGREDIENTS	IMPERIAL	METRIC	AMERICAN
Butter	2 oz	50 g	$\frac{1}{4}$ cup
Chicken joints	4	4	4
Medium onion, chopped	1	1	1
Mushrooms, sliced	8 oz	225 g	2 cups
Medium dry sherry	$\frac{1}{4}$ pt	150 ml	$\frac{2}{3}$ cup
Salt			
Black pepper			
Double/thick cream	$\frac{1}{2}$ pt	300 ml	$1\frac{1}{4}$ cups
Paprika	$\frac{1}{2}$–1 tsp	$\frac{1}{2}$–1 tsp	$\frac{1}{2}$–1 tsp
Chopped fresh parsley	2 tbsp	2 tbsp	2 tbsp

Heat the butter in the open pressure cooker and brown the chicken joints well on all sides. Remove. In the same butter sauté the onion gently for 2–3 minutes. Stir in the mushrooms and sherry and season with salt and pepper. Bring to pressure and cook for given time. Reduce pressure.

Lift the chicken joints on to a serving dish and keep warm. Stir the remaining ingredients into the sherry mixture. Adjust seasoning if necessary then reheat, without boiling, and pour over the chicken.

COOKING TIME High/15-lb pressure 7 minutes
Reduce pressure quickly

SERVES 4

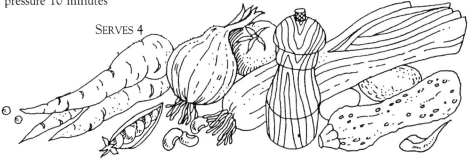

CHICKEN RISOTTO

INGREDIENTS	IMPERIAL	METRIC	AMERICAN
Butter	3 oz	75 g	6 tbsp
Onions, chopped	2	2	2
Clove garlic, crushed (optional)	1	1	1
Green pepper, de-seeded and chopped	1	1	1
Mushrooms, sliced	4 oz	100 g	1 cup
Cooked chicken, chopped	8 oz	225 g	$\frac{1}{2}$ lb
Long-grain rice	8 oz	225 g	$1-1\frac{1}{4}$ cups
White wine	$\frac{1}{4}$ pt	150 ml	$\frac{2}{3}$ cup
Chicken stock	$\frac{3}{4}$ pt	400 ml	2 cups
Salt and pepper			
Grated Parmesan cheese			

Heat the butter in the open pressure cooker and sauté the onions, garlic, pepper and mushrooms for a few minutes. Stir in the cooked chicken, rice, wine and chicken stock. Season to taste. Bring to pressure and cook for given time. Reduce pressure.

Place the open pressure cooker on a gentle heat and fluff up the rice with a fork to separate the grains. Sprinkle with Parmesan cheese and serve.

COOKING TIME High/15-lb pressure 5 minutes
Reduce pressure slowly

NOTE Risotto may be made using any cooked meat or fish.

SERVES 4

CHICKEN ITALIENNE

INGREDIENTS	IMPERIAL	METRIC	AMERICAN
Butter	2 oz	50 g	$\frac{1}{4}$ cup
Chicken thighs	8	8	8
Cloves garlic, crushed	2	2	2
Onions, chopped	2	2	2
Streaky bacon, chopped	4 oz	100 g	$\frac{1}{4}$ lb
Tomatoes, skinned and sliced	4	4	4
Mushrooms, sliced	4 oz	100 g	1 cup
Tomato purée/paste	4 tbsp	4 tbsp	4 tbsp
Chicken stock	$\frac{3}{4}$ pt	400 ml	2 cups
Dried oregano	1 tsp	1 tsp	1 tsp
Salt and pepper			
Flour	2 tbsp	2 tbsp	2 tbsp

Heat the butter in the open pressure cooker and brown the chicken on all sides. Remove it from the pressure cooker. In the same butter, sauté the garlic, onions and bacon gently for about 2 minutes. Stir in the tomatoes, mushrooms, tomato purée, chicken stock, oregano and seasoning. Return the chicken to pressure cooker, bring to pressure and cook for given time. Reduce pressure.

Mix the flour with a little cold water to form a smooth paste and stir it into the chicken. Bring to the boil, stirring continuously.

COOKING TIME High/15-lb pressure 7 minutes
Reduce pressure quickly

SERVES 4

CHICKEN WITH ALMONDS AND SPICES

INGREDIENTS	IMPERIAL	METRIC	AMERICAN
Olive oil	2 tbsp	2 tbsp	2 tbsp
Onion, thinly sliced	1	1	1
Chicken quarters, skinned	4	4	4
Ground cinnamon	$\frac{1}{2}$ tsp	$\frac{1}{2}$ tsp	$\frac{1}{2}$ tsp
Ground ginger	$\frac{1}{2}$ tsp	$\frac{1}{2}$ tsp	$\frac{1}{2}$ tsp
Pinch saffron thread soaked in a little wine or water			
Blanched almonds	4 oz	100 g	1 cup
Chicken stock	$\frac{1}{2}$ pt	300 ml	$1\frac{1}{4}$ cups
Unsalted butter, diced (optional)	$1\frac{1}{2}$ oz	40 g	3 tbsp
Large bunch fresh coriander or parsley, finely chopped			
Salt and pepper			
Lightly toasted flaked almonds, to garnish			

Heat the oil in the open pressure cooker and sauté the onion, stirring occasionally, until softened but not coloured. Add the chicken and cook for 2–3 minutes. Remove and keep warm. Stir the cinnamon, ginger and saffron, with its soaking liquor, into the onion and cook, stirring, for 2 minutes. Stir in the almonds and stock, add the chicken. Bring to pressure and cook for given time. Reduce pressure. Lift out the chicken and remove the flesh from the bones.

Meanwhile, boil the cooking liquor hard in the open pressure cooker until well reduced. Reduce the heat to very low then gradually whisk in the butter, if used.

Left: Chicken with Almonds and Spices. Right: Pork with Wine and Coriander (page 32).

Return the chicken to the liquor, stir in the coriander or parsley, adjust the seasoning and spices and serve with the flaked almonds scattered over.

COOKING TIME High/15-lb pressure 6 minutes
Reduce pressure quickly

SERVES 4

CHICKEN AVGOLOMONO

INGREDIENTS	IMPERIAL	METRIC	AMERICAN
Juice of $\frac{1}{2}$ lemon			
Chicken breasts, skinned	4	4	4
Chicken stock	$\frac{1}{2}$ pt	300 ml	$1\frac{1}{4}$ cups
Bouquet garni	1	1	1
Egg yolks, beaten	3	3	3
Lemon juice	4 tbsp	4 tbsp	4 tbsp
Salt and white pepper			
Sprigs of parsley, to garnish			

Squeeze lemon juice over both sides of the chicken; leave for 30 minutes, if possible.

Pour the stock into the cooker and add the bouquet garni and chicken. Bring to pressure and cook for given time. Reduce pressure.

Transfer the chicken to a warmed serving plate and keep warm. Boil the cooking juices in the open cooker until reduced to 7 fl oz/200 ml/scant cup. Remove the bouquet garni. Blend the egg yolks and lemon juice together in a bowl. Whisk in a little of the reduced cooking juices then pour back into the cooker. Cook over a low heat, stirring with a wooden spoon, until thickened. Do not allow to boil. Adjust the seasoning, pour through a sieve over the chicken and garnish.

COOKING TIME High/15-lb pressure 4 minutes
Reduce pressure slowly

NOTE Make the bouquet garni with 1 bay leaf, a sprig of parsley, sprig of thyme and rosemary.

SERVES 4

CHICKEN PAPRIKA

INGREDIENTS	IMPERIAL	METRIC	AMERICAN
Chicken portions	4	4	4
Olive oil	2 tbsp	2 tbsp	2tbsp
Onions, sliced	2	2	2
Tomatoes, skinned and sliced	4	4	4
Clove garlic, crushed	1	1	1
Button mushrooms	4 oz	100 g	1 cup
Paprika	1 tbsp	1 tbsp	1 tbsp
Chicken stock	$\frac{1}{2}$ pt	300 ml	$1\frac{1}{4}$ cups
Flour	2 tbsp	2 tbsp	2 tbsp
Salt and pepper			

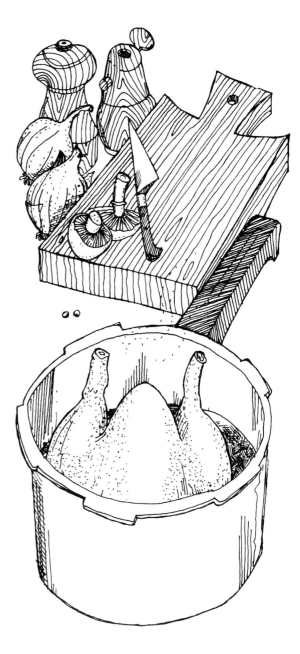

Trim the chicken joints. Heat the oil in the open pressure cooker and fry the chicken portions until lightly browned on all sides. Remove from the cooker.

Add the onions, tomatoes, garlic, mushrooms and paprika to the cooker and fry for a few minutes. Return the chicken and add the stock. Bring to pressure and cook for given time. Reduce pressure.

Remove the chicken from the cooker and place on a warm serving dish, keep hot. Blend the flour with a little cold water and stir into the cooker with seasoning to taste. Bring to the boil and simmer for 2 minutes. Pour over the chicken.

COOKING TIME High/15-lb pressure 7 minutes
Reduce pressure quickly

SERVES 4

STUFFED PEPPERS

INGREDIENTS	IMPERIAL	METRIC	AMERICAN
Medium green peppers	4	4	4
Cooked chicken, chopped	8 oz	225 g	$\frac{1}{2}$ lb
Small onions, chopped	2	2	2
Streaky bacon/bacon slices, chopped	4 oz	100 g	$\frac{1}{4}$ lb
Cooked long-grain rice	12 oz	350 g	$\frac{3}{4}$ lb
Ground cumin	1 tsp	1 tsp	1 tsp
Salt and pepper			

Cut off the stem end of the peppers and scoop out the seeds. Mix together the remaining ingredients, seasoning well. Fill each pepper with equal portions of the stuffing mixture. Pour $\frac{1}{2}$ pt/300 ml/1$\frac{1}{4}$ cups water into the pressure cooker and position the trivet. Stand the stuffed peppers on the trivet, bring to pressure and cook for given time. Reduce pressure. Lift the peppers on to a serving dish and garnish them with a few crispy grilled/broiled pieces of bacon, if liked.

COOKING TIME High/15-lb pressure 4 minutes
Reduce pressure quickly

NOTE When reducing pressure, take care not to tilt the pressure cooker, causing the peppers to topple and the stuffing to spill out.

SERVES 4

CAULIFLOWER NIÇOISE

INGREDIENTS	IMPERIAL	METRIC	AMERICAN
Cooking oil	1 tbsp	1 tbsp	1 tbsp
Butter	1 oz	25 g	2 tbsp
Onion, chopped	1	1	1
Clove garlic, crushed	1	1	1
Cauliflower, cut into florets	1	1	1
Can tomatoes	14 oz	397 g	1 lb
Chicken stock	$\frac{1}{4}$ pt	150 ml	$\frac{2}{3}$ cup
Dried basil	$\frac{1}{2}$–1 tsp	$\frac{1}{2}$–1 tsp	$\frac{1}{2}$–1 tsp
Salt and pepper			
Black olives, stoned/pitted	6–8	6–8	6–8

Heat the oil and butter in the open pressure cooker and sauté the onion and garlic until transparent. Stir in the remaining ingredients, bring to pressure and cook for given time. Reduce pressure.

COOKING TIME High/15-lb pressure 5 minutes
Reduce pressure quickly

SERVES 4

FAR EASTERN
COOKERY

The subtle flavours of Oriental cookery are enhanced by pressure cooking. Succulent Chinese dishes, like Red cooked pork and Sweet and sour pork, are delicious and both cook in under 5 minutes. Using your pressure cooker for popular Rogan josh or delicious Zaffrani murgh – chicken with saffron and spices – makes the preparation of an Indian meal so easy. Far Eastern cookery can transform familiar meat, fish, poultry and vegetables into the most exotic dishes.

CHICKEN SATAY

INGREDIENTS	IMPERIAL	METRIC	AMERICAN
Chicken breasts, skinned and cut into large cubes	$1\frac{1}{4}$ lb	550 g	$1\frac{1}{4}$ lb
Small onions, finely diced	2	2	2
Peanut or groundnut oil	2 fl oz	50 ml	$\frac{1}{4}$ cup
Cardamom pods, crushed	2	2	2
Allspice berries, crushed	2	2	2
Coriander seeds, crushed	1 tsp	1 tsp	1 tsp
Fennel seeds, crushed	$\frac{1}{2}$ tsp	$\frac{1}{2}$ tsp	$\frac{1}{2}$ tsp
Garam masala	$\frac{1}{2}$ tsp	$\frac{1}{2}$ tsp	$\frac{1}{2}$ tsp
Juice of 1 lemon, and rind pared in long strips, finely sliced			
Chicken stock	$\frac{1}{2}$ pt	300 ml	$1\frac{1}{4}$ cups
Clove garlic, crushed	1	1	1
Fresh root ginger, peeled and very finely chopped	1 oz	25 g	1 oz
Crunchy peanut butter	4 oz	100 g	$\frac{1}{2}$ cup
Block creamed coconut, chopped	2 oz	50 g	2 oz
Salt and pepper			
Lime juice			

Put the chicken into a bowl. Mix 1 onion with the oil, spices, and lemon, pour over the chicken and fold it over gently to coat. Cover and leave in the refrigerator for about 8 hours.

Remove the chicken from the bowl and thread on to short skewers or satay sticks.

Pour the stock into the pressure cooker and add the remaining onion and the garlic. Oil the trivet and put in place. Put the chicken on the trivet in a single layer; trim the sticks, if necessary, to fit them all in without stacking them. Bring to pressure and cook for given time. Reduce pressure.

Transfer the chicken to a warmed serving dish and keep warm. Add the ginger to the stock and boil until reduced by half. Purée with the peanut butter and coconut. Add seasoning and lime juice, to taste. Warm through gently then serve with the chicken.

COOKING TIME High/15-lb pressure $2\frac{1}{2}$ minutes
Reduce pressure quickly

SERVES 4–6

DHAL SOUP WITH SPICY YOGURT

INGREDIENTS	IMPERIAL	METRIC	AMERICAN
Ghee or oil	2 tbsp	2 tbsp	2 tbsp
Small onion, diced	1	1	1
Cloves garlic, finely chopped	2	2	2
Piece fresh root ginger, peeled and finely chopped	1 inch	2.5 cm	1 inch
Bay leaf	1	1	1
Cumin seeds, finely crushed	$\frac{1}{2}$–1 tsp	$\frac{1}{2}$–1 tsp	$\frac{1}{2}$–1 tsp
Cloves, bruised	2	2	2
Yellow split peas	8 oz	225 g	$\frac{1}{2}$ lb
Celery sticks	2	2	2
Leek, chopped	1	1	1
Carrot, diced	1	1	1
Vegetable stock	2 pt	1.1 l	5 cups
Grated rind and juice of 1 lemon			
Salt and pepper			
Chopped coriander leaves, to garnish			

Spiced Yogurt:			
Plain yogurt	4 fl oz	100 ml	$\frac{1}{2}$ cup
Paprika pepper	$\frac{1}{2}$ tsp	$\frac{1}{2}$ tsp	$\frac{1}{2}$ tsp
Ground turmeric	$\frac{1}{2}$ tsp	$\frac{1}{2}$ tsp	$\frac{1}{2}$ tsp
Ground cumin	$\frac{1}{4}$ tsp	$\frac{1}{4}$ tsp	$\frac{1}{4}$ tsp
Cayenne	$\frac{1}{4}$ tsp	$\frac{1}{4}$ tsp	$\frac{1}{4}$ tsp
Salt			

Heat the ghee or oil in the open pressure cooker and cook the onion, garlic, ginger, bay leaf, cumin and cloves over a moderately low heat, stirring occasionally, for 3–4 minutes. Stir in the split peas, celery, leek and carrot, cook for 1–2 minutes then stir in the stock. Bring to the boil, skim the scum from the surface, adjust the heat so the contents just boil but do not rise. Bring to pressure over the same heat and cook for given time.

For the spiced yogurt, whisk the yogurt until smooth then stir in the remaining ingredients.

Reduce pressure. Remove and discard the bay leaf. Purée the soup, return to the cooker and add the lemon rind and juice and seasoning to taste; adjust the flavourings and consistency, if necessary. Heat through gently. Serve in warmed bowls topped with a spoonful of the spiced yogurt and a sprinkling of coriander leaves.

COOKING TIME High/15-lb pressure 5 minutes
Reduce pressure slowly

SERVES 4–6

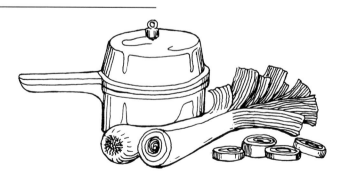

DHAL

INGREDIENTS	IMPERIAL	METRIC	AMERICAN
Ghee or oil	2 tbsp	2 tbsp	2 tbsp
Onion, cut into rings	1	1	1
Cloves garlic, chopped	3	3	3
Onion seeds	$\frac{1}{2}$ tsp	$\frac{1}{2}$ tsp	$\frac{1}{2}$ tsp
Ground turmeric	$\frac{1}{4}$ tsp	$\frac{1}{4}$ tsp	$\frac{1}{4}$ tsp
Green chilli, sliced	1	1	1
Dried red chilli, slightly slit	1	1	1
Cumin seeds	$\frac{1}{2}$ tsp	$\frac{1}{2}$ tsp	$\frac{1}{2}$ tsp
Red lentils	8 oz	225 g	$\frac{1}{2}$ lb
Vegetable stock	1 pt	550 ml	$2\frac{1}{2}$ cups

Heat the ghee or oil in the open pressure cooker over a medium heat and sauté the onion, stirring occasionally, until browned. Add the garlic. Cook for 1–2 minutes then stir in the onion seeds. Cook until they begin to pop then stir in the turmeric, chilli, cumin and lentils. Stir for 1–2 minutes. Add the stock, bring to the boil in the open cooker over a low heat and skim the scum from the surface. Reduce the heat so the contents are boiling but not rising in the pan. Maintaining the same heat, bring to pressure and cook for given time. Reduce pressure.

Strain the lentils and keep warm. Boil the cooking liquid in the open cooker until almost completely evaporated, then stir back into the lentils.

COOKING TIME Low/5-lb pressure 4 minutes
Reduce pressure slowly

SERVES 4

PILAU

INGREDIENTS	IMPERIAL	METRIC	AMERICAN
Ghee or oil	3 tbsp	3 tbsp	3 tbsp
Onion, finely chopped	1	1	1
Clove garlic, crushed	1	1	1
Cloves	4	4	4
Cardamom pods	8	8	8
Piece cinnamon stick	2 inch	5 cm	2 inch
Bay leaves	2	2	2
Long-grain rice	8 oz	225 g	generous 1 cup
Chicken or vegetable stock, or water	$1\frac{1}{2}$ pt	900 ml	$3\frac{3}{4}$ cups
Shelled pistachio nuts, peeled	2 oz	50 g	$\frac{1}{3}$ cup
Sultanas/white raisins	2 oz	50 g	$\frac{1}{3}$ cup
Salt and pepper			
Orange flower water (optional)			

Heat 2 tbsp of the ghee or oil in the open pressure cooker and fry the onion, stirring occasionally, until browned. Stir in the garlic and cook for 1–2 minutes. Crush the cloves, cardamom pods and cinnamon together and add to the cooker with the bay leaves and rice. Cook, stirring for 2–3 minutes. Stir in the stock or water. Bring to pressure and cook for given time.

Meanwhile, heat the remaining oil in a pan and fry the nuts until golden.

Reduce pressure. Strain the rice, remove the spices and bay leaves, return the rice to the rinsed cooker over a very low heat and fluff up the rice with a fork, adding the nuts and sultanas at the same time. Season and add orange flower water to taste if used.

COOKING TIME High/15-lb pressure 2 minutes
Reduce pressure slowly

SERVES 4

BRAISED PORK WITH GINGER

INGREDIENTS	IMPERIAL	METRIC	AMERICAN
Cooking oil	3 tbsp	3 tbsp	3 tbsp
Finely chopped fresh root ginger	1 tbsp	1 tbsp	1 tbsp
Cloves garlic, crushed	2	2	2
Finely chopped spring onion/scallion	3 tbsp	3 tbsp	3 tbsp
Rice wine	2 tbsp	2 tbsp	2 tbsp
Dark soy sauce	2 tbsp	2 tbsp	2 tbsp
Brown sugar	2 tsp	2 tsp	2 tsp
Lean pork, cut into large cubes	$1\frac{1}{4}$ lb	550 g	$1\frac{1}{4}$ lb
Chicken stock	14 fl oz	400 ml	$1\frac{3}{4}$ cups
Cornflour/cornstarch	2 tsp	2 tsp	2 tsp
Dry roasted sesame seeds	1–2 tbsp	1–2 tbsp	1–2 tbsp

Mix together half of the oil, the ginger, garlic, spring onion, rice wine, soy sauce and brown sugar. Add the pork, stirring it to coat in the marinade. Cover and leave in a cool place for about 4 hours.

Heat the remaining oil in the open pressure cooker to just below smoking point. Add half of the pork and cook until evenly browned. Remove, using a slotted spoon. Repeat with the remaining pork. Place all the meat in the cooker, stir in any remaining marinade and the stock. Bring to pressure and cook for given time. Reduce pressure.

Blend the cornflour with a little water, stir into the cooker and bring to the boil, stirring. Cook until thickened slightly. Scatter the sesame seeds over.

COOKING TIME High/15-lb pressure 4 minutes
Reduce pressure slowly

SERVES 4

CHICKEN CURRY

INGREDIENTS	IMPERIAL	METRIC	AMERICAN
Coriander seeds	1 tbsp	1 tbsp	1 tbsp
Cumin seeds	1 tbsp	1 tbsp	1 tbsp
Fresh root ginger, peeled	1 inch	2.5 cm	1 inch
Ground turmeric	2 tsp	2 tsp	2 tsp
Chilli powder	2 tsp	2 tsp	2 tsp
Garam masala	2 tsp	2 tsp	2 tsp
Ghee or oil	3 tbsp	3 tbsp	3 tbsp
Chicken portions	4	4	4
Large onion, thinly sliced	1	1	1
Cloves garlic, crushed	4	4	4
Chicken stock	12 fl oz	350 ml	$1\frac{1}{2}$ cups

Heat the coriander and cumin in a small, heavy pan for 2–3 minutes. Pound with the ginger then work in the turmeric, chilli powder, garam masala and half of the ghee or oil. Spread over the chicken, cover and leave in a cool place for 3 hours.

Heat the remaining ghee or oil in the open pressure cooker and sauté the chicken, onion and garlic and cook over a fairly high heat to lightly colour the outside of the chicken. Add the stock. Bring to pressure and cook for given time. Reduce pressure (see Note).

Remove the chicken and keep warm. Boil the liquid to thicken the sauce. Lower the heat and add the chicken, turning it over in the sauce to coat evenly.

COOKING TIME High/15-lb pressure 6 minutes
Reduce pressure quickly

NOTE If left to cool, then covered and kept in a cool place overnight, the flavours will mature and combine to give a fuller flavoured dish. Reheat thoroughly.

SERVES 4

Left: Braised Pork with Ginger. Right: Chicken Curry.

CHINESE LEMON CHICKEN

INGREDIENTS	IMPERIAL	METRIC	AMERICAN
Soy sauce	1½ tbsp	1½ tbsp	1½ tbsp
Oyster sauce	1½ tbsp	1½ tbsp	1½ tbsp
Cooking oil	1½ tbsp	1½ tbsp	1½ tbsp
Chicken	3½ lb	1.6 kg	3½ lb
Chinese chicken stock (see page 48)	15 fl oz	425 ml	scant 2 cups
Dried Chinese mushrooms, stems removed, caps sliced	4	4	4
Piece fresh root ginger, peeled and cut into thin strips	1¼ inch	3 cm	1¼ inch
Large lemon, thinly sliced	1	1	1
Cornflour/cornstarch	2 tsp	2 tsp	2 tsp
Lemon juice	2 tbsp	2 tbsp	2 tbsp
Salt and white pepper			
Granulated sugar			
Cashew nuts and watercress, to garnish			

Mix the soy and oyster sauces and oil together then spread over the chicken. Leave for 1 hour.

Pour the stock into the pressure cooker and add the mushrooms. Put the trivet in place then place chicken on the trivet. Sprinkle the ginger over and put some in the cavity, then cover the bird with the lemon slices, put any remaining in the cavity. Bring to pressure and cook for given time. Reduce pressure.

Transfer the chicken to a warmed serving plate. Remove the mushrooms from the liquid. Boil the liquid in the open cooker until reduced to 7 fl oz/200 ml/scant 1 cup. Blend the cornflour with the lemon juice then stir into the cooker. Bring to the boil, stirring, and boil until thickened slightly. Taste and adjust the seasoning, adding a little sugar, if necessary.

Remove the lemon slices from the chicken and pour the sauce over. Scatter cashew nuts over, if liked, and serve with the mushrooms and watercress.

COOKING TIME High/15-lb pressure 20 minutes
Reduce pressure slowly

NOTE Photograph on page 2.

SERVES 4

CHINESE CHICKEN STOCK

INGREDIENTS	IMPERIAL	METRIC	AMERICAN
Chicken, jointed	3 lb	1.4 kg	3 lb
Water	2 pt	1.1 l	5 cups
Mixed carrots, celery, spring onions/ scallions, leeks, roughly chopped	12 oz	350 g	¾ lb
Piece fresh root ginger, peeled and cut into pieces	1 inch	2.5 cm	1 inch
Soy sauce	2 tsp	2 tsp	2 tsp

Put the chicken and water into the pressure cooker. Bring to pressure and cook for 30 minutes. Reduce pressure.

Add the vegetables, return to pressure and cook for 5 minutes. Reduce pressure. Add the ginger and soy sauce, return to pressure and cook for given time.

Reduce pressure, strain off the liquid and leave to cool. Remove the fat from the surface. Cover and refrigerate the stock.

COOKING TIME High/15-lb pressure chicken 30 minutes
  vegetables added 5 minutes
  soy sauce and ginger added 2 minutes
Reduce pressure quickly

MAKES 2 pt/1.1l/5 cups

ZAFFRANI MURGH
(Chicken with Saffron and Spices)

INGREDIENTS	IMPERIAL	METRIC	AMERICAN
Saffron threads	$\frac{1}{2}$ tsp	$\frac{1}{2}$ tsp	$\frac{1}{2}$ tsp
Piece fresh root ginger, peeled and finely chopped	2 inch	5 cm	2 inch
Cinnamon stick, broken	2 inch	5 cm	2 inch
Whole cardamom pods, lightly crushed	6	6	6
Cloves, lightly crushed	6	6	6
Ground coriander seeds	1 tbsp	1 tbsp	1 tbsp
Ground cumin seeds	1 tbsp	1 tbsp	1 tbsp
Cayenne pepper	$\frac{1}{2}$ tsp	$\frac{1}{2}$ tsp	$\frac{1}{2}$ tsp
Ghee, clarified butter or oil	2 tbsp	2 tbsp	2 tbsp
Plain yogurt	12 fl oz	350 ml	$1\frac{1}{2}$ cups
Bay leaves, torn	2	2	2
Large onion, sliced	1	1	1
Cloves garlic, crushed	2	2	2
Large chicken leg portions, skinned	4	4	4
Cornflour/cornstarch	1 tsp	1 tsp	1 tsp
Block creamed coconut, chopped	1 oz	25 g	1 oz
Salt and pepper			
Sprigs of fresh coriander or flat-leafed parsley, to garnish			

In a small, heavy pan, heat the spices for about 3 minutes. Remove from the heat and stir in the ghee, yogurt, bay leaves, onion and garlic.

Place the chicken in a non-metallic dish that it just fits, pour the spiced yogurt mixture over, turning the chicken in the yogurt to coat completely. Cover the dish and leave in a cool place for about 4 hours.

Remove the chicken from the marinade, allowing excess to drain off. Blend the cornflour with 2 tbsp water then stir in the marinade. Pour into the pressure cooker, over a very low heat, stirring slowly in one direction. Bring to just on simmering point then simmer gently, still stirring slowly, for a few minutes. Turn the chicken in the yogurt to coat it. Bring to pressure and cook for given time. Reduce pressure.

Transfer the chicken to a warmed serving dish and keep warm. Over a low heat, stir the coconut into the cooking juices. Heat gently, stirring, for 2–3 minutes. Adjust the seasonings and flavourings. Divide the chicken legs into drumsticks and thighs then stir them into the cooker to coat in the sauce. Serve scattered with fresh coriander or flat-leafed parsley sprigs.

COOKING TIME High/15-lb pressure 5 minutes
Reduce pressure quickly

SERVES 4

ROGAN JOSH

INGREDIENTS	IMPERIAL	METRIC	AMERICAN
Cornflour/cornstarch	1 tsp	1 tsp	1 tsp
Plain yogurt	12 fl oz	350 ml	1½ cups
Ghee or oil	3 tbsp	3 tbsp	3 tbsp
Large onion, thinly sliced	1	1	1
Cloves garlic, crushed	3	3	3
Piece fresh root ginger, peeled and finely chopped	1 inch	2.5 cm	1 inch
Ground coriander	1 tbsp	1 tbsp	1 tbsp
Ground cumin	2 tsp	2 tsp	2 tsp
Ground cardamom	2 tsp	2 tsp	2 tsp
Ground chilli powder	1 tsp	1 tsp	1 tsp
Ground cloves	1 tsp	1 tsp	1 tsp
Tomato purée/paste	1 tbsp	1 tbsp	1 tbsp
Lean lamb, cut into large cubes	1¼ lb	550 g	1¼ lb
Ground almonds	3–4 tbsp	3–4 tbsp	3–4 tbsp
Fresh coriander leaves	2 tbsp	2 tbsp	2 tbsp

Blend the cornflour with 2 tbsp water. Stir in the yogurt then heat very gently, stirring very slowly in one direction, until just on simmering point. Simmer gently, stirring in the same way, for a few minutes. Pour from the cooker.

Heat half of the ghee or oil in the pressure cooker, add the onion and cook until lightly browned. Add the garlic, cook for 1–2 minutes then stir in the spices and tomato purée. Remove from the heat and stir in the yogurt. Place the lamb in a non-metallic dish that it just fits, pour the spiced yogurt over, turning the meat to coat evenly. Cover and leave in a cool place for 4 hours.

Remove the meat from the marinade, allowing the excess to drain off. Heat the remaining ghee or oil in the pressure cooker, add the lamb and cook, stirring, for 1–2 minutes, then stir in the marinade. Slowly bring to pressure and cook for given time. Reduce pressure.

Remove the meat and keep warm. Stir the ground almonds into the cooking juices and heat gently until thickened slightly. Lower the heat and add the coriander leaves. Stir the meat back into the sauce to coat it evenly and adjust the seasoning.

COOKING TIME High/15-lb pressure 3 minutes
Reduce pressure quickly

SERVES 4

RED COOKED PORK

INGREDIENTS	IMPERIAL	METRIC	AMERICAN
Belly of pork with skin	1½ lb	700 g	1½ lb
Slices fresh root ginger	3	3	3
Dark soy sauce	3 tbsp	3 tbsp	3 tbsp
Brown sugar	2 tsp	2 tsp	2 tsp
Chinese chicken stock (see page 48)	14 fl oz	400 ml	1¾ cups
Red food colouring (optional)			

Cut the pork into approximately 2 inch/5 cm long pieces, discarding any bone. Put into the pressure cooker with all the ingredients, except the food colouring. Stir well, then bring to pressure and cook for given time. Reduce pressure. (See Note.)

Remove the pork using a slotted spoon and keep warm. Boil the cooking juices in the open cooker until well reduced to make a thickish sauce. Return the pork to the cooker and stir over a low heat to coat with the sauce. Add a few drops of red food colouring, if liked.

COOKING TIME High/15-lb pressure 4½ minutes
Reduce pressure slowly

NOTE If left, covered, in a cool place overnight, the flavours of this dish will mature and combine, giving it a richer, fuller flavour. Reheat thoroughly.

SERVES 4

Above: Rogan Josh. Below: Red Cooked Pork.

BRAISED LAMB

INGREDIENTS	IMPERIAL	METRIC	AMERICAN
Fresh root ginger, peeled	1 oz	25 g	1 oz
Large spring onions/scallions, halved crosswise	4	4	4
Whole star anise	1	1	1
Piece cinnamon	1 inch	2.5 cm	1 inch
Veal stock	14 fl oz	400 ml	$1\frac{3}{4}$ cups
Dark soy sauce	2 tbsp	2 tbsp	2 tbsp
Brown sugar	2 tsp	2 tsp	2 tsp
Lean lamb, cut into large cubes	$1\frac{1}{4}$ lb	550 g	$1\frac{1}{4}$ lb
Sesame oil, to taste			
Chopped spring onions/scallions, to serve			

Cut the ginger into several chunks, place on a board and bang them with a rolling pin. Put into the pressure cooker with the spring onions, spices, stock, soy sauce and sugar. Stir in the lamb. Bring to pressure and cook for given time. Reduce pressure. (See Note.)

Using a slotted spoon, remove the lamb and keep warm. Boil the cooking liquid in the open cooker to concentrate the flavours – taste to check the balance. Discard the spices then return the lamb to the cooker and stir to coat in the liquid. Sprinkle sesame oil over the lamb and serve with chopped spring onions scattered over.

COOKING TIME High/15-lb pressure $4\frac{1}{2}$ minutes
Reduce pressure slowly

NOTE If left, covered, in a cool place overnight, the flavours of this dish will mature and combine together, giving it a richer, fuller flavour.

SERVES 4

CHICKEN WINGS IN BLACK BEAN SAUCE

INGREDIENTS	IMPERIAL	METRIC	AMERICAN
Cooking oil	$1\frac{1}{2}$ tbsp	$1\frac{1}{2}$ tbsp	$1\frac{1}{2}$ tbsp
Chopped fresh root ginger	$1\frac{1}{2}$ tbsp	$1\frac{1}{2}$ tbsp	$1\frac{1}{2}$ tbsp
Clove garlic, crushed	1	1	1
Spring onions/scallions, finely chopped	2	2	2
Chopped black beans	2 tbsp	2 tbsp	2 tbsp
Dark soy sauce	2 tbsp	2 tbsp	2 tbsp
Rice wine or dry sherry	2 tbsp	2 tbsp	2 tbsp
Brown sugar	$1\frac{1}{2}$ tsp	$1\frac{1}{2}$ tsp	$1\frac{1}{2}$ tsp
Chicken wings	8	8	8
Chinese chicken stock (see page 48)	7 fl oz	200 ml	scant 1 cup
Cornflour/cornstarch	2 tsp	2 tsp	2 tsp
Sesame oil (optional)	1 tbsp	1 tbsp	1 tbsp

Heat the oil in a pan and cook the ginger and garlic for 2 minutes. Stir in the spring onions, black beans, soy sauce, rice wine or sherry and sugar and simmer for a further 2 minutes. Put the chicken into a dish, pour the sauce over, turning the chicken over to coat in the sauce. Leave for about 1 hour.

Pour the chicken stock into the pressure cooker, add the chicken and marinade. Bring to pressure and cook for given time. Reduce pressure.

Blend the cornflour with the sesame oil, if used, and a little water. Stir into the cooker and bring to the boil, stirring. Boil until thickened slightly. Turn the chicken wings in the sauce to coat them. Serve sprinkled with a little extra sesame oil, if liked.

COOKING TIME High/15-lb pressure 2 minutes
Reduce pressure quickly

SERVES 4

BEEF CURRY

INGREDIENTS	IMPERIAL	METRIC	AMERICAN
Butter	3 oz	75 g	6 tbsp
Each, ground coriander, cumin, chillies, cardamom, turmeric	1½ tsp	1½ tsp	1½ tsp
Each, ground ginger, fenugreek, pepper, mixed spice	½ tsp	½ tsp	½ tsp
Clove garlic, crushed	1	1	1
Large onion, chopped	1	1	1
Stewing steak, cut into cubes	1½ lb	700 g	1½ lb
Cinnamon stick	1	1	1
Bay leaf	1	1	1
Beef stock	½ pt	300 ml	1¼ cups
Juice of ½ lemon			
Caster/superfine sugar	1 tbsp	1 tbsp	1 tbsp
Long-grain rice	8 oz	225 g	1–1¼ cups
Slightly salted boiling water	¾ pt	400 ml	2 cups

Heat the butter in the open pressure cooker and fry the dry spices gently with the garlic for 2–3 minutes. Add the onion and sauté until soft. Add the cubes of meat and stir until they are covered with spices and beginning to brown.

Stir in the remaining ingredients, except the rice and water, bring to pressure and cook for given time. Reduce pressure.

Put the rice into an ovenproof bowl, pour the boiling water over it and cover securely with foil. Place the trivet on the meat and stand the bowl on the trivet. Bring to pressure again and cook for given time. Reduce pressure.

Fluff up the rice with a fork to separate the grains and arrange it on a warmed serving dish.

Remove the bay leaf and cinnamon stick from the curry. If liked, the curry may be thickened with a little cornflour mixed with cold water. Spoon the curry into the centre of the rice. Serve with some of the following: thinly sliced tomato and onion; sliced bananas, sprinkled with lemon juice; cucumber cubes dressed with plain yogurt; chutney.

COOKING TIME High/15-lb pressure curry 15 minutes
Reduce pressure quickly
    rice added 5 minutes
Reduce pressure slowly

NOTE If preferred, the dry spices may be replaced with 2–3 tbsp curry powder.

SERVES 4–6

VEGETABLE CURRY

INGREDIENTS	IMPERIAL	METRIC	AMERICAN
Mustard seeds	3 tsp	3 tsp	3 tsp
Coriander seeds	3 tsp	3 tsp	3 tsp
Cumin seeds	3 tsp	3 tsp	3 tsp
Ghee or oil	3 tbsp	3 tbsp	3 tbsp
Large onion, halved and thinly sliced	1	1	1
Cloves garlic, crushed	2	2	2
Piece fresh root ginger, peeled and thinly sliced	1 inch	2.5 cm	1 inch
Ground turmeric	1½ tsp	1½ tsp	1½ tsp
Chilli powder	1½ tsp	1½ tsp	1½ tsp
Can tomatoes, juice made up to ½ pt/ 300 ml/1¼ cups with vegetable stock or water	14 oz	397 g	1 lb
Tomato purée/paste	2 tsp	2 tsp	2 tsp
Potatoes, cut into large chunks	12 oz	350 g	¾ lb
Carrots, cut into large chunks	8 oz	225 g	½ lb
Courgettes/zucchini, cut into chunks	8 oz	225 g	½ lb
Small cauliflower, broken into florets	1	1	1
Block creamed coconut, chopped	1½ oz	40 g	1½ oz
Salt and pepper			

Heat the mustard seeds, coriander seeds and cumin seeds together in a small, heavy, non-stick saucepan for 2–3 minutes, shaking the pan occasionally. Crush finely.

Heat the ghee or oil in the open pressure cooker and gently fry the onion and garlic, stirring occasionally, until softened. Add the ginger and continue to cook until the onion is just beginning to colour. Stir in the crushed spices, with the turmeric and chilli powder. Cook gently for 2–3 minutes, then stir in the tomatoes and the tomato juice, tomato purée, potatoes and carrots. Bring to pressure and cook for 1½ minutes. Reduce pressure. Add the courgettes and cauliflower, bring to pressure and cook for given time. Reduce pressure.

Strain off the liquid and reserve. Transfer the vegetables to a warmed serving dish and return the liquid to the cooker. Boil hard in the open cooker until reduced to about 6 fl oz/175 ml/¾ cup. Reduce the heat and stir in the coconut. Continue to stir over a low heat for a few minutes. Adjust the seasoning and flavourings, if necessary. Gently stir in the vegetables and coat them with the sauce.

COOKING TIME High/15-lb pressure first vegetables
1½ minutes
courgettes and cauliflower added 1½ minutes
Reduce pressure quickly

SERVES 4

TROUT WITH GINGER AND SPRING ONIONS

INGREDIENTS	IMPERIAL	METRIC	AMERICAN
Lemon juice	2 tbsp	2 tbsp	2 tbsp
Light soy sauce	3 tbsp	3 tbsp	3 tbsp
Finely chopped peeled fresh root ginger	1½ tsp	1½ tsp	1½ tsp
Spring onions/scallions, trimmed, 2 finely chopped, 2 cut into strips	4	4	4
Cloves garlic, very finely chopped	2	2	2
Black pepper			
Trout, filleted	4	4	4
Fish stock (see page 60)	8 fl oz	250 ml	1 cup
Cornflour/cornstarch	2 tsp	2 tsp	2 tsp
Olive oil	2 tsp	2 tsp	2 tsp
Carrot, cut into thin strips	1	1	1
Courgette/zucchini, cut into strips	1	1	1
Mangetout/snow peas, cut into thin strips	2 oz	50 g	2 oz

Mix 1 tbsp each lemon juice and soy sauce, the ginger, chopped spring onions and 1 garlic clove and a little black pepper together. Rub the mixture into the fish. Pour the stock and remaining soy and lemon juice into the pressure cooker and put the oiled trivet in place. Fold the fillets in half and place on the trivet. Bring to pressure and cook for given time. Reduce pressure.

Transfer the trout to a warmed serving plate and keep warm. Remove the trivet. Blend the cornflour with any remaining marinade, or water, pour into the cooker then bring to the boil, stirring. Cook, still stirring, until thickened slightly. Adjust the level of flavourings, if necessary.

Meanwhile, heat the oil in a non-stick pan and cook the remaining garlic briefly, stirring. Add the remaining spring onions and other vegetables and cook, stirring, for about 3 minutes until crisp and bright. Using a slotted spoon, remove and place on kitchen paper. Pour the sauce over and around the fish and scatter the spring onions, carrot, courgette and mangetout over.

COOKING TIME High/15-lb pressure 2 minutes
Reduce pressure quickly

SERVES 4

SWEET AND SOUR PORK

INGREDIENTS	IMPERIAL	METRIC	AMERICAN
Rice wine	2 tbsp	2 tbsp	2 tbsp
Light soy sauce	3 tbsp	3 tbsp	3 tbsp
Cooking oil	3 tbsp	3 tbsp	3 tbsp
Chinese five spice powder	1 tsp	1 tsp	1 tsp
Tomato purée/paste	2 tsp	2 tsp	2 tsp
Grated fresh root ginger	$1\frac{1}{2}$ tsp	$1\frac{1}{2}$ tsp	$1\frac{1}{2}$ tsp
Onion, finely chopped	1	1	1
Cloves garlic, finely crushed	2	2	2
Lean pork, cut into large cubes	1 lb	450 g	1 lb
Red pepper, de-seeded, chopped	$\frac{1}{2}$	$\frac{1}{2}$	$\frac{1}{2}$
Green pepper, de-seeded, chopped	$\frac{1}{2}$	$\frac{1}{2}$	$\frac{1}{2}$
Chinese chicken stock (see page 48)	8 fl oz	250 ml	1 cup
Brown sugar	$1\frac{1}{2}$ tsp	$1\frac{1}{2}$ tsp	$1\frac{1}{2}$ tsp
Cornflour/cornstarch	2 tsp	2 tsp	2 tsp

Mix together the rice wine, soy sauce, a third of the oil, the five spice powder, tomato purée, ginger, onion and garlic. Add the pork and stir it around gently to coat evenly. Cover and leave in a cool place for 2 hours.

Heat the remaining oil in the open pressure cooker and sauté the peppers, stirring occasionally, for 2 minutes. Using a slotted spoon, transfer to kitchen paper. Remove the pork from the marinade and add to the cooker. Cook, stirring, for 2–3 minutes. Stir in the remaining marinade, the stock and sugar. Bring to pressure and cook for given time. Reduce pressure.

Remove the pork and keep warm. Add the peppers and cornflour blended with a little water to the cooker and boil, stirring, without the lid, until slightly thick-ened. Adjust the flavourings, lower the heat, add the pork and stir to coat in the sauce.

COOKING TIME High/15-lb pressure 4 minutes
Reduce pressure quickly

SERVES 4

CHICKEN CHOW MEIN

INGREDIENTS	IMPERIAL	METRIC	AMERICAN
Boneless chicken breasts	12 oz	350 g	$\frac{3}{4}$ lb
Cooking oil	4 tbsp	4 tbsp	4 tbsp
Onion, sliced	1	1	1
Celery, sliced	6 oz	175 g	$1\frac{1}{2}$ cups
Fresh bean sprouts	6 oz	175 g	3 cups
Mushrooms, sliced	8 oz	225 g	2 cups
Chinese chicken stock (see page 48)	$\frac{1}{2}$ pt	300 ml	$1\frac{1}{4}$ cups
Honey	1 tbsp	1 tbsp	1 tbsp
Soy sauce	4 tbsp	4 tbsp	4 tbsp

Cut the raw chicken breast meat into bite-sized pieces. Heat the oil in the open pressure cooker, add the chicken and fry quickly until lightly browned. Remove with a slotted spoon. Add the onion, celery, bean sprouts and mushrooms to the remaining oil in the pressure cooker and fry until lightly browned.

Return the chicken to the cooker with the stock, honey and soy sauce. Bring to pressure and cook for given time. Reduce pressure. Serve with crispy fried noodles or boiled rice. Serve extra soy sauce separately.

COOKING TIME High/15-lb pressure 5 minutes
Reduce pressure quickly

SERVES 4

SPICED PEAS

INGREDIENTS	IMPERIAL	METRIC	AMERICAN
Ghee or oil	3 tbsp	3 tbsp	3 tbsp
Large onion, halved and thinly sliced	1	1	1
Cumin seeds, lightly crushed	1 tsp	1 tsp	1 tsp
Fresh shelled young peas (about 2 lb/900 g/2 lb peas in the pod)	12 oz	350 g	$\frac{3}{4}$ lb
Green chilli, de-seeded, chopped	1	1	1
Vegetable stock or water (optional)	4 tbsp	4 tbsp	4 tbsp
Small bunch fresh coriander, chopped			
Salt and pepper			

Heat the ghee or oil in the open pressure cooker and gently fry the onion and cumin, stirring occasionally, until the onion is beginning to colour. Stir in the peas, chilli and stock. Line the separator basket with oiled foil, pour in the contents of the cooker then cover with foil. Place the trivet in the cooker, pour in $\frac{1}{2}$ pt/300 ml/ 11/4 cups water then stand the basket on the trivet. Bring to pressure and cook for given time. Reduce pressure.

Stir the coriander into the peas. Adjust the seasoning, if necessary, then pour, with the cooking juices, into a warmed serving dish.

COOKING TIME High/15-lb pressure 7–8 minutes
Reduce pressure quickly

SERVES 4

SEAFOOD

There are several advantages of cooking fish in your pressure cooker. Though the time saving will not be great, since fish is quickly cooked by most methods, you will appreciate the full flavour of pressure-cooked fish. (Bring the pressure cooker up to pressure quickly or the fish will cook before the cooker is up to pressure.) Hardly any flavour is lost if the minimum amount of liquid is used, and the fish is cooked in the steam. Make sure you retain the flavour and nutritive value by using the cooking liquor to make a delicious accompanying sauce.

Fish keeps its shape very well in the pressure cooker. Wrap in buttered foil to enable easy removal from the pressure cooker.

A great advantage is that fishy odours – those characteristic smells that float around the house informing everyone that fish is definitely for dinner – are reduced to a minimum. These are sealed inside the pressure cooker until the last minute.

Various types of fish are available today and most can be substituted for those given in the recipes. Try the less expensive coley to replace cod or haddock, for instance.

SALMON WITH FENNEL

INGREDIENTS	IMPERIAL	METRIC	AMERICAN
Vegetable stock	$\frac{1}{2}$ pt	300 ml	1$\frac{1}{4}$ cups
White pepper			
Salmon steaks	4	4	4
Trimmed fennel bulbs, quartered, feathery tops reserved	10 oz	275 g	10 oz
Fromage blanc	1$\frac{1}{2}$ oz	40 g	3 tbsp
Salt			
Lemon juice			
Anise-flavoured liquor eg Ricard (optional)			

Oil the trivet and place in the pressure cooker. Pour the stock into the cooker. Sprinkle freshly ground white pepper over the salmon then place on the trivet. Put the fennel into the basket and place over the salmon. Bring to pressure and cook for given time. Reduce pressure.

Lift out the basket. Transfer the salmon to a warmed serving dish and keep warm. Boil the cooking liquor hard until reduced to about 4 tbsp. Purée the fennel with the reduced stock and fromage blanc. Heat through gently in a small saucepan, stirring, but do not allow to boil. Season with salt and white pepper and add a little lemon juice and anise liquor, if necessary. Pour the sauce around the salmon and garnish with the reserved feathery fennel tops.

COOKING TIME High/15-lb pressure 3 minutes
Reduce pressure quickly

SERVES 4

FISH STOCK

INGREDIENTS	IMPERIAL	METRIC	AMERICAN
Unsalted butter, diced	$\frac{3}{4}$ oz	20 g	$1\frac{1}{2}$ tbsp
Small onion, cut in half	1	1	1
Small leek, white part only, chopped	1	1	1
Button or cup mushrooms, chopped	$1\frac{1}{2}$ oz	40 g	$\frac{1}{3}$ cup
Fish bones, heads and trimmings, soaked in cold water for 3 hours, drained	$1\frac{3}{4}$ lb	1 kg	$1\frac{3}{4}$ lb
Medium-bodied dry white wine	$\frac{1}{4}$ pt	150 ml	$\frac{2}{3}$ cup
Bouquet garni (see Note)	1	1	1

Heat the butter in the open pressure cooker and add all the vegetables. Cover and cook over a moderate heat, shaking the cooker occasionally, for 4–5 minutes. Add the fish bones and trimmings and cook for a further 2–3 minutes. Stir in the wine and boil until reduced by half. Add the bouquet garni followed by $1\frac{1}{2}$ pt/900 ml/$3\frac{3}{4}$ cups water. Bring to the boil and skim the scum from the surface. Bring to pressure and cook for given time. Reduce pressure.

Strain the stock through a sieve lined with muslin/cheesecloth and leave to cool. Remove the fat from the surface, then cover and keep in the refrigerator.

COOKING TIME High/15-lb pressure 10 minutes
Reduce pressure slowly

NOTE Make bouquet garni from 1 bay leaf, 3 parsley stalks and a sprig of fennel.
MAKES ABOUT $1\frac{1}{2}$ pt/900 ml/$3\frac{3}{4}$ cups.

COD COUNTRY STYLE

INGREDIENTS	IMPERIAL	METRIC	AMERICAN
Cod steaks	4	4	4
Butter	3 oz	75 g	6 tbsp
Salt and pepper			
Juice 1 lemon			
Clove garlic, crushed	1	1	1
Potatoes, thinly sliced	4	4	4
Onions, sliced	2	2	2
Can tomatoes	14 oz	397 g	1 lb
Water	$\frac{1}{4}$ pt	150 ml	$\frac{2}{3}$ cup
Good pinch thyme			
Few sprigs of parsley			

Place each cod steak on a separate piece of foil. Dot each with butter, using 25 g/1 oz, season and sprinkle with lemon juice. Fold the foil over each steak and seal to form four parcels.

Heat the remaining butter in the open pressure cooker and sauté the garlic, potatoes and onions for 2–3 minutes, seasoning well. Add the tomatoes, including the juice, water and thyme. Place the trivet on the vegetables then the cod parcels on top. Bring to pressure and cook for given time. Reduce pressure. Lift out the fish parcels and the trivet. Arrange the vegetables on a serving dish. Open the foil parcels and place the cod steaks on top of the vegetables. Pour any juice from the parcels over the steaks and garnish each with a sprig of parsley.

COOKING TIME High/15-lb pressure 5 minutes
Reduce pressure quickly

SERVES 4

WAITAKI FISH SCALLOPS

INGREDIENTS	IMPERIAL	METRIC	AMERICAN
Cod, haddock or hake fillets	1 lb	450 g	1 lb
Medium onion	1	1	1
Bay leaf	1	1	1
Parsley			
Salt	1 tsp	1 tsp	1 tsp
Few peppercorns			
Malt vinegar	1 tsp	1 tsp	1 tsp
Water	$\frac{1}{2}$ pt	300 ml	$1\frac{1}{4}$ cups
Sauce: Butter	3 tbsp	3 tbsp	3 tbsp
Flour	$1\frac{1}{2}$ oz	40 g	$\frac{1}{3}$ cup
Milk	$\frac{1}{4}$ pt	150 ml	$\frac{2}{3}$ cup
Fish liquor	$\frac{1}{2}$ pt	300 ml	$1\frac{1}{4}$ cups
Cheese, grated	4 oz	100 g	1 cup
Lemon juice			
Salt and pepper			
Mustard and cress and lemon butterflies, to garnish			

Place the fish, whole onion, bay leaf, parsley, salt and peppercorns, vinegar and water in the pressure cooker, without the trivet. Bring to pressure and cook for given time. Reduce pressure. Lift out the fish, skin and flake it, then chop the onion. Strain the fish liquor. Wipe out the pressure cooker with kitchen paper.

To make the sauce, melt the butter in the open pressure cooker and sauté the chopped onion gently for a few minutes. Remove from the heat and stir in the flour. When smooth, add the milk gradually and stir in $\frac{1}{2}$ pt/300 ml/$1\frac{1}{4}$ cups of the fish liquor (add water to make up the quantity if necessary). Cook gently for 3–5 minutes. Remove from the heat and stir in three-quarters of the cheese, seasoning to taste with lemon juice, salt and pepper. Thin it, if necessary, with a little more fish liquor.

Take four scallop shells or small ovenproof dishes and place a large spoonful of sauce on each. Divide the fish between the four shells, then cover the fish with the remaining sauce. Sprinkle it with the remaining grated cheese and brown under a hot grill/broiler. Just before serving, garnish with mustard and cress or watercress and lemon butterflies.

COOKING TIME High/15-lb pressure 4 minutes
Reduce pressure quickly

SERVES 4

MONKFISH AND ARTICHOKE RAGOUT

INGREDIENTS	IMPERIAL	METRIC	AMERICAN
Fresh globe artichoke bottoms, freshly prepared	4	4	4
Lemon juice			
Olive oil	2 tbsp	2 tbsp	2 tbsp
Onion, finely chopped	1	1	1
Cloves garlic, chopped	4	4	4
Monkfish steaks, cut across the bone	4	4	4
Medium dry white wine	8 fl oz	250 ml	1 cup
Can tomatoes	14 oz	397 g	1 lb
Sun-dried tomatoes, chopped (see Note)	3	3	3
Bay leaf	1	1	1
Large black olives, stoned/pitted	10	10	10
Black pepper			
Capers	1 tbsp	1 tbsp	1 tbsp

Cut each artichoke bottom into quarters, then cut each quarter in four. Toss immediately in lemon juice.

Heat the oil in the open pressure cooker and gently cook the onion and garlic until softened but not coloured. Add the artichoke quarters and cook, stirring occasionally, for 2–3 minutes. Add the fish, wine, tomatoes, dried tomatoes and bay leaf. Bring to pressure and cook for given time. Reduce pressure.

Transfer the fish to a warmed serving dish and keep warm. Add the olives to the cooker and boil rapidly in the open cooker to reduce and thicken the sauce. Remove the bay leaf. Season with pepper. Return the fish to the cooker. Serve sprinkled with capers.

Above: Monkfish and Artichoke Ragout. Below: Soused Herrings.

COOKING TIME High/15-lb pressure $2\frac{1}{2}$ minutes
Reduce pressure quickly

NOTE If sun-dried tomatoes are not available, add tomato purée/paste to taste.

SERVES 4

SOUSED HERRINGS

INGREDIENTS	IMPERIAL	METRIC	AMERICAN
Small herrings	8	8	8
Salt and pepper			
Dried red chilli	1	1	1
Blade mace	1	1	1
Bay leaf	1	1	1
Whole allspice	3	3	3
Black peppercorns	6	6	6
Small onions, thinly sliced	1–2	1–2	1–2
Malt vinegar	$\frac{1}{4}$ pt	150 ml	$\frac{2}{3}$ cup
Water	$\frac{1}{4}$ pt	150 ml	$\frac{2}{3}$ cup

Scale and clean the herrings, removing the heads and tails. Split and bone the fish. Lightly season the fillets on the fleshy side with salt and pepper. Roll each up from the tail end, skin side outside, and secure each roll with a wooden cocktail stick/toothpick. Place the herrings in the pressure cooker without the trivet and add the remaining ingredients. Bring to pressure and cook for given time. Reduce pressure.

Arrange the herrings in a serving dish and pour the liquor over the fish. Allow it to cool and serve as a starter or with a salad and boiled potatoes as a main dish.

COOKING TIME High/15-lb pressure 6 minutes
Reduce pressure quickly

NOTE Boned mackerel or pilchards may also be prepared in this way.

SERVES 4

WARM MONKFISH AND CELERIAC SALAD

INGREDIENTS	IMPERIAL	METRIC	AMERICAN
Celeriac, depending how thickly it is peeled	$1\frac{1}{2}$ lb	700 g	$1\frac{1}{2}$ lb
Lemon juice			
Monkfish fillet, cut into large chunks	$1\frac{1}{2}$ lb	700 g	$1\frac{1}{2}$ lb
Vegetable stock	$\frac{1}{2}$ pt	300 ml	$1\frac{1}{4}$ cups
Egg yolk	1	1	1
Grated rind and juice of 1 lemon			
Wholegrain mustard	1 tbsp	1 tbsp	1 tbsp
Olive oil	$3\frac{1}{2}$ fl oz	100 ml	scant $\frac{1}{2}$ cup
Whipping cream, lightly whipped	$2\frac{1}{2}$ fl oz	70 ml	5 tbsp

Peel the celeriac, cut into cubes and immediately toss in lemon juice. Put the monkfish, celeriac and stock into the pressure cooker, without the trivet. Bring to pressure and cook for given time. Reduce pressure.

Remove the fish and celeriac and keep warm. Boil half of the stock in the open cooker until reduced by half.

Whisk the egg yolk, 1 tsp lemon juice and the mustard together in a small bowl until well mixed. Gradually whisk in the oil to form a thick mayonnaise, then beat in the reduced stock and lemon rind. Lastly, fold in the cream. Season and adjust the acidity and level of mustard. Divide the monkfish into smaller pieces, then mix with the celeriac. Spoon the dressing over and toss briefly.

COOKING TIME High/15-lb pressure 2 minutes
Reduce pressure quickly

SERVES 4

HADDOCK IN CREOLE SAUCE

INGREDIENTS	IMPERIAL	METRIC	AMERICAN
Cooking oil	2 tbsp	2 tbsp	2 tbsp
Small onion, chopped	1	1	1
Clove garlic, crushed	1	1	1
Celery stick, chopped	1	1	1
Green pepper, de-seeded and chopped	1	1	1
Can tomatoes	14 oz	397 g	1 lb
Tomato purée/paste	1 tbsp	1 tbsp	1 tbsp
Sugar	1 tsp	1 tsp	1 tsp
Pinch basil			
Chilli powder	$\frac{1}{2}$ tsp	$\frac{1}{2}$ tsp	$\frac{1}{2}$ tsp
Salt and pepper			
Haddock fillets, skinned and cut into cubes	4	4	4

Heat the oil in the open pressure cooker and sauté the onion, garlic, celery and pepper gently for 2–3 minutes. Stir in the tomatoes, including the juice made up to $\frac{1}{2}$ pt/300 ml/$1\frac{1}{4}$ cups with water. Add the tomato purée, sugar, basil, chilli powder, seasoning and haddock pieces. Bring to pressure and cook for given time. Reduce pressure.

COOKING TIME High/15-lb pressure 4 minutes
Reduce pressure quickly

NOTE This recipe is equally good made with prawns/shrimp. Replace the haddock with 8 oz/225 g peeled prawns and cook for 3 minutes at High/15-lb pressure.

SERVES 4

SMOKED HADDOCK CASSEROLE

INGREDIENTS	IMPERIAL	METRIC	AMERICAN
Butter	1 oz	25 g	2 tbsp
Onions, chopped	2	2	2
Tomatoes, skinned and sliced	4	4	4
Frozen peas	4 oz	100 g	$\frac{1}{4}$ lb
Smoked haddock, skinned, cut into cubes	$1\frac{1}{2}$ lb	700 g	$1\frac{1}{2}$ lb
Pinch ground mace			
Sugar	2 tsp	2 tsp	2 tsp
Salt and pepper			
Water	$\frac{3}{4}$ pt	400 ml	2 cups
Flour	1 oz	25 g	$\frac{1}{4}$ cup
Milk	$\frac{1}{4}$ pt	150 ml	$\frac{2}{3}$ cup
Chopped fresh parsley, to garnish			

Heat the butter in the open pressure cooker and sauté the onions until transparent. Stir in the tomatoes, peas, smoked haddock, mace, sugar, seasoning and water. Bring to pressure and cook for given time. Reduce pressure.

Mix the flour with the milk to form a smooth paste and add it to the fish. Bring to the boil, stirring gently. Sprinkle with a little chopped parsley just before serving.

COOKING TIME High/15-lb pressure 3 minutes
Reduce pressure quickly

SERVES 4

HADDOCK WITH PESTO SAUCE

INGREDIENTS	IMPERIAL	METRIC	AMERICAN
Milk	$\frac{1}{2}$ pt	300 ml	$1\frac{1}{4}$ cups
Shallot, finely chopped	1	1	1
Haddock steaks	4	4	4
Black pepper			
Lemon juice			
Unsalted butter	1 oz	25 g	2 tbsp
Plain/all-purpose flour	1 oz	25 g	$\frac{1}{4}$ cup
Pesto Sauce (see Note)	2 tbsp	2 tbsp	2 tbsp
Tomatoes, skinned and chopped	2	2	2

Pour the milk into the pressure cooker and add the shallot. Season the haddock steaks with pepper and lemon juice and place them on the oiled trivet. Bring to pressure and cook for given time. Reduce pressure.

Transfer the haddock to a warmed serving plate. Remove the trivet from the cooker and pour out the milk and shallot. Reserve. Melt the butter in a saucepan, add the reserved shallot and cook for about 2 minutes. Stir in the flour and cook for 2 minutes, stirring. Remove from the heat and gradually stir in the reserved milk, keeping the mixture smooth. Return to the heat and bring to the boil, stirring. Simmer for 2–3 minutes. Remove from the heat and whisk in the pesto. Adjust the seasoning and pour over the fish. Scatter the tomato over the top.

COOKING TIME High/15-lb pressure $2\frac{1}{2}$ minutes
Reduce pressure quickly

NOTE Pesto sauce, made from fresh basil, garlic and cheese, can be prepared at home or bought, in bottles or jars, from delicatessens and supermarkets.

SERVES 4

SOLE FILLETS WITH MUSHROOMS

INGREDIENTS	IMPERIAL	METRIC	AMERICAN
Olive oil			
Sole fillets, skinned	8	8	8
Lemon juice			
Black pepper			
Cottage cheese, drained and sieved	6 oz	175 g	$\frac{3}{4}$ cup
Finely grated rind of 1 lemon			
Salt			
Dash Tabasco sauce			
Peeled prawns/shrimp, roughly chopped	$1\frac{1}{2}$ oz	40 g	$\frac{1}{4}$ cup
Medium dry white wine	$\frac{1}{4}$ pt	150 ml	$\frac{2}{3}$ cup
Button mushrooms, chopped	8 oz	225 g	2 cups
Chopped fresh tarragon or $\frac{1}{2}$ tsp dried	1 tsp	1 tsp	1 tsp
Fromage blanc	$1\frac{1}{2}$ oz	40 g	3 tbsp
Sprigs of tarragon and cooked prawns/shrimp, to garnish			

Brush the trivet with oil. Sprinkle both sides of each sole fillet with a little lemon juice and pepper. Lay half of the fillets flat on the trivet, with the skinned side facing uppermost. Mash the cottage cheese with the lemon rind, a little salt and a dash of Tabasco to taste, then stir in the prawns. Divide half of the cheese mixture between the fillets on the trivet, roll them up and secure with cocktail sticks/toothpicks. Repeat with the remaining fillets.

Pour $\frac{1}{4}$ pt/150 ml/$\frac{2}{3}$ cup water and the wine into the pressure cooker and put the trivet in place. Put the mushrooms in the basket and place over the fish. Bring to pressure and cook for given time. Reduce pressure.

Transfer the fish to a warmed serving dish, discard the cocktail sticks and keep the fish warm. Boil the cooking liquor hard in the open cooker until reduced to 3 tbsp. Purée the mushrooms coarsely with the tarragon, reduced cooking liquor and fromage blanc, to give a rough texture. Heat through gently in a small saucepan, stirring, without allowing to boil. Adjust the seasoning and add a little lemon juice, if necessary, to lift the flavour. Serve with the fish. Garnish with sprigs of tarragon and cooked prawns.

COOKING TIME High/15-lb pressure $2\frac{1}{2}$ minutes
Reduce pressure quickly

SERVES 4

DEVON HADDOCK

INGREDIENTS	IMPERIAL	METRIC	AMERICAN
Haddock fillets, skinned and cut into cubes	4	4	4
Seasoned flour			
Butter	1 oz	25 g	2 tbsp
Onions, chopped	2	2	2
Carrots, sliced	2	2	2
Green pepper, de-seeded and sliced	1	1	1
Cider	1 pt	550 ml	$2\frac{1}{2}$ cups
Bay leaf	1	1	1
Chopped fresh parsley	1 tbsp	1 tbsp	1 tbsp

Coat the haddock pieces with a little seasoned flour. Heat the butter in the open pressure cooker and sauté the vegetables lightly for 2–3 minutes. Stir in the haddock, then the cider. Add the bay leaf. Bring to pressure and cook for given time. Reduce pressure. Remove the bay leaf and adjust seasoning if necessary. Stir in the chopped parsley just before serving.

COOKING TIME High/15-lb pressure 4 minutes
Reduce pressure slowly

SERVES 4

TUNA FISH IN TOMATO AND MUSHROOM SAUCE

INGREDIENTS	IMPERIAL	METRIC	AMERICAN
Can tuna fish	7 oz	198 g	$\frac{1}{2}$ lb
Lemon juice	2 tsp	2 tsp	2 tsp
Pinch dried basil			
Cooking oil	2 tbsp	2 tbsp	2 tbsp
Onions, chopped	2	2	2
Mushrooms, sliced	4 oz	100 g	1 cup
Can tomatoes	14 oz	397 g	1 lb
Water	$\frac{1}{4}$ pt	150 ml	$\frac{2}{3}$ cup
Sherry (optional)	2 tbsp	2 tbsp	2 tbsp
Mustard	2 tsp	2 tsp	2 tsp
Salt and pepper			

Sprinkle the tuna with the lemon juice and basil, then flake the fish with a fork. Heat the oil in the open pressure cooker and sauté the onions until transparent. Stir in the remaining ingredients, bring to pressure and cook for given time. Reduce pressure.

If liked, thicken the sauce with a little flour mixed with cold water. Serve with buttered noodles or spaghetti.

COOKING TIME High/15-lb pressure 5 minutes
Reduce pressure quickly

SERVES 4

APPLE SOLE

INGREDIENTS	IMPERIAL	METRIC	AMERICAN
Fillets sole	6	6	6
Salt and pepper			
Apple juice	$\frac{1}{2}$ pt	300 ml	$1\frac{1}{4}$ cups
Cornflour/cornstarch	2 tsp	2 tsp	2 tsp
Single/thin cream	$\frac{1}{4}$ pt	150 ml	$\frac{2}{3}$ cup
Chopped fresh parsley			

Season the sole fillets and roll them up, skin side inside. Arrange the rolls in the pressure cooker without the trivet and pour the apple juice around them. Bring to pressure and cook for given time. Reduce pressure.

Lift the fish rolls on to a warmed serving dish. Mix the cornflour with a little cold water to form a smooth paste and add it to the apple juice. Bring to the boil, stirring well. Stir in the cream, reheat the sauce gently and pour it over the fish. Sprinkle with a little chopped parsley and serve.

COOKING TIME High/15-lb pressure 4 minutes
Reduce pressure quickly

CHECKPOINT Do not boil the sauce when reheating or the cream will separate.

SERVES 4

PIQUANT PLAICE

INGREDIENTS	IMPERIAL	METRIC	AMERICAN
Plaice fillets	$1\frac{1}{2}$ lb	700 g	$1\frac{1}{2}$ lb
Salt and pepper			
Butter	1 oz	25 g	2 tbsp
Small onion, chopped	1	1	1
Clove garlic, crushed	1	1	1
Tomato purée/paste	2 tbsp	2 tbsp	2 tbsp
Worcestershire sauce	2 tsp	2 tsp	2 tsp
Sugar	$\frac{1}{2}$ tsp	$\frac{1}{2}$ tsp	$\frac{1}{2}$ tsp
Water	$\frac{1}{2}$ pt	300 ml	$1\frac{1}{4}$ cups
Cornflour/cornstarch	1 tbsp	1 tbsp	1 tbsp
Lemon wedges, to garnish			

Skin the plaice fillets and season with salt and pepper. Roll them up and secure each with wooden cocktail sticks/toothpicks. Heat the butter in the open pressure cooker and sauté the onion and garlic gently until transparent. Add remaining ingredients, except the cornflour and lemon wedges, and stir well. Sit the plaice rolls in the sauce. Bring to pressure and cook for given time. Reduce pressure.

Arrange the plaice rolls on a warmed serving dish. Mix the cornflour with a little cold water to form a smooth paste and add it to the sauce. Bring to the boil, stirring well. Pour over and around the plaice and garnish with lemon wedges.

COOKING TIME High/15-lb pressure 4 minutes
Reduce pressure quickly

SERVES 4

STUFFED MACKEREL

INGREDIENTS	IMPERIAL	METRIC	AMERICAN
Mackerel, cleaned	4	4	4
Salt and pepper			
Eating apples, grated	2	2	2
Small onion, finely chopped	1	1	1
Fresh white breadcrumbs	2 oz	50 g	1 cup
Cheddar cheese, grated	4 oz	100 g	1 cup
Butter, melted	2–3 oz	50–75 g	$\frac{1}{4} - \frac{1}{3}$ cup
Lemon twists and chopped fresh parsley, to garnish			

Wipe the inside of the mackerel and season it inside and out with salt and pepper. Mix together the apple, onion, breadcrumbs and grated cheese. Season to taste, then bind the mixture with 2 tbsp of the melted butter. Stuff the fish and secure it with wooden cocktail sticks/toothpicks. Place each fish on a separate sheet of foil. Pour the remaining melted butter over the mackerel. Fold the foil over and seal it to make four parcels.

Pour $\frac{1}{2}$ pt/300 ml/$1\frac{1}{4}$ cups water into the pressure cooker and position the trivet. Place the parcels on the trivet. Bring to pressure and cook for given time. Reduce pressure.

Open the parcels and arrange the mackerel on a warmed serving dish. Pour any butter left in the foil over the fish and garnish them with lemon twists and parsley.

COOKING TIME High/15-lb pressure 6 minutes
Reduce pressure quickly

NOTE Herring is also excellent cooked this way.

SERVES 4

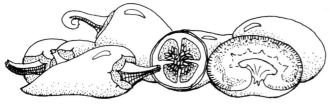

VEGETARIAN
COOKERY

As vegetables are cooked in steam in a pressure cooker, the colour, flavour, texture and nutrients are retained. Another plus for vegetarians is that pulses – dried peas, beans and lentils – need only 1 hour soaking in boiling water before speedy pressure cooking; unlike the lengthy process of soaking overnight required if boiling them in the usual way. Pulses are an important part of a vegetarian diet as they are a rich source of protein. This chapter contains a host of exciting, new recipes for soups, snacks and both light and main vegetarian dishes.

BORLOTTI BEAN AND FENNEL SALAD

INGREDIENTS	IMPERIAL	METRIC	AMERICAN
Borlotti beans	4 oz	100 g	$\frac{1}{4}$ lb
Olive oil	4 tbsp	4 tbsp	4 tbsp
Lemon juice	2 tbsp	2 tbsp	2 tbsp
Finely chopped fresh parsley	1 tbsp	1 tbsp	1 tbsp
Meaux mustard	$1\frac{1}{2}$ tsp	$1\frac{1}{2}$ tsp	$1\frac{1}{2}$ tsp
Clove garlic, finely crushed	1	1	1
Salt and pepper			
Small fennel bulb, thinly sliced	1	1	1
Feta or goats' cheese, crumbled	4 oz	100 g	$\frac{1}{4}$ lb
Crisp lettuce leaves			
Slices rye, Granary or wholemeal bread, cut into cubes, baked or fried until crisp	1–2	1–2	1–2

Pour boiling water over the beans and leave to soak for 1 hour. Drain the beans then put into the open pressure cooker with 1 pt/550 ml/2$\frac{1}{2}$ cups water. Bring to the boil, remove the scum from the surface and adjust the heat, so the contents boil but do not rise. Bring to pressure and cook for given time. Reduce pressure.

Strain the beans. Whisk the oil, lemon juice, parsley, mustard, garlic and seasoning together and stir into the beans while they are still warm. Leave to cool, then toss with the fennel and cheese. Place the lettuce in a shallow bowl and add the bean salad. Scatter the bread cubes over and toss in lightly.

COOKING TIME High/15-lb pressure 10 minutes
Reduce pressure slowly

SERVES 4

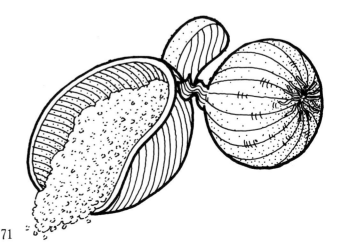

VEGETABLE STOCK

INGREDIENTS	IMPERIAL	METRIC	AMERICAN
Unsalted butter, chopped	$\frac{3}{4}$ oz	20 g	$1\frac{1}{2}$ tbsp
Small shallots, diced	2	2	2
Small leek, white part only, chopped	1	1	1
Small carrot, chopped	1	1	1
Chopped fennel or fennel seeds	$1\frac{1}{2}$ tbsp $\frac{3}{4}$ tsp	$1\frac{1}{2}$ tbsp $\frac{3}{4}$ tsp	$1\frac{1}{2}$ tbsp $\frac{3}{4}$ tsp
Mushroom peelings			
Small tomatoes, chopped	2	2	2
Bouquet garni (see Note)	1	1	1
White peppercorns, crushed	$\frac{3}{4}$ tsp	$\frac{3}{4}$ tsp	$\frac{3}{4}$ tsp

Heat the butter in the open pressure cooker, add the shallots and leek, cover and cook over a low heat, shaking the cooker occasionally, until soft. Stir in the remaining ingredients and add $1\frac{1}{2}$ pt/900 ml/$3\frac{3}{4}$ cups water. Bring to the boil and skim the scum from the surface. Bring to pressure and cook for given time. Reduce pressure.

Strain the stock through a sieve lined with muslin/cheesecloth, then leave to cool. Remove the fat from the surface, cover and store in the refrigerator.

COOKING TIME High/15-lb pressure 4 minutes
Reduce pressure slowly

NOTE Make bouquet garni using 4 parsley stalks, 1 bay leaf, a sprig of chervil and thyme.
MAKES ABOUT $1\frac{1}{2}$ pt/900 ml/$3\frac{3}{4}$ cups

CREAM OF CAULIFLOWER SOUP

INGREDIENTS	IMPERIAL	METRIC	AMERICAN
Medium cauliflower, chopped	1	1	1
Vegetable stock	$1\frac{1}{2}$ pt	900 ml	$3\frac{3}{4}$ cups
Butter	1 oz	25 g	2 tbsp
Salt and pepper			
Pinch grated nutmeg			
Single/thin cream	$\frac{1}{4}$ pt	150 ml	$\frac{2}{3}$ cup

Place all the ingredients, except the cream, into the pressure cooker. Bring to pressure and cook for given time. Reduce pressure. Purée the soup and return it to the pressure cooker. Reheat and stir in the cream just before serving.

COOKING TIME High/15-lb pressure 4 minutes
Reduce pressure slowly

CHECKPOINT Do not boil the soup after adding the cream.

SERVES 4

PASTA AND SPAGHETTI SOUP

INGREDIENTS	IMPERIAL	METRIC	AMERICAN
Haricot/navy beans	3 oz	75 g	$\frac{1}{2}$ cup
Olive oil	3 tbsp	3 tbsp	3 tbsp
Onion, finely chopped	1	1	1
Cloves garlic, finely crushed	3	3	3
Small carrot, finely chopped	1	1	1
Stick celery, finely chopped	1	1	1
Tomatoes, skinned and chopped	3	3	3
Vegetable stock	2 pt	1.1 l	5 cups
Tomato purée/paste	2 tsp	2 tsp	2 tsp
Spaghetti, broken into about 1 inch/2.5 cm lengths	2 oz	50 g	2 oz
Basil leaves, torn	8–10	8–10	8–10
Salt and pepper			
Finely chopped parsley and freshly grated Parmesan cheese, to serve			

Pour boiling water over the beans and leave to soak for 1 hour. Heat the oil in the open pressure cooker and gently fry the onion, garlic, carrot and celery, stirring occasionally, until softened but not coloured. Drain the beans and add to the cooker with the tomatoes. Pour in the stock and add the tomato purée. Bring to the boil in the open cooker, adjust the heat so the contents are boiling but not rising in the pan. Bring to pressure over the same heat and cook for given time. Reduce pressure.

Remove and reserve about half to two-thirds of the beans and a ladleful of the liquor. Bring the open cooker to the boil, add the spaghetti and stir. Bring to pressure over a medium heat and cook for given time.

Purée the reserved beans and liquor. Reduce pressure. Stir the puréed beans into the cooker and simmer for 2–3 minutes to thicken. Add the basil and season to taste. Serve sprinkled with plenty of finely chopped parsley and freshly grated Parmesan.

COOKING TIME High/15-lb pressure beans 15 minutes spaghetti added $1\frac{1}{2}$ minutes
Reduce pressure slowly

SERVES 6

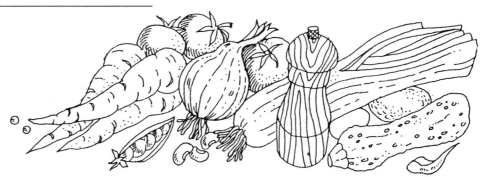

TRIPLE LAYERED GRATIN

INGREDIENTS	IMPERIAL	METRIC	AMERICAN
Carrots, chopped	12 oz	350 g	$\frac{3}{4}$ lb
Small parsnips, chopped	12 oz	350 g	$\frac{3}{4}$ lb
Medium Brussels sprouts	12 oz	350 g	$\frac{3}{4}$ lb
Salt and pepper			
Finely grated rind and juice 1 small orange (optional)			
Finely chopped fresh root ginger (optional)	1 tsp	1 tsp	1 tsp
Squeeze of lemon juice	1 tsp	1 tsp	1 tsp
Unsalted butter, diced	75 g	3 oz	6 tbsp
Piece of goats' cheese, sliced	4 oz	100 g	$\frac{1}{4}$ lb

Put the trivet into the pressure cooker and pour in $\frac{1}{2}$ pt/300 ml/1$\frac{1}{4}$ cups water. Place the vegetables in the separator on the trivet, keeping them separate. Bring to pressure and cook for given time. Reduce pressure.

Purée the vegetables separately, seasoning each one and adding, to taste, orange rind and juice to the carrots, ginger to the parsnips and lemon juice to the sprouts, if liked. Add about half of the butter to the parsnips and a half of the remainder each to the carrots and sprouts.

Spread the carrot purée in an even layer in a buttered heatproof dish, parsnip purée and lastly the sprouts. Cover the top with the slices of cheese, sprinkle with black pepper and place under a hot grill/broiler until bubbling and lightly browned.

COOKING TIME High/15-lb pressure 3 minutes
Reduce pressure quickly

SERVES 4

QUICK VEGETABLE RAGOUT

INGREDIENTS	IMPERIAL	METRIC	AMERICAN
Celeriac	1 lb	450 g	1 lb
Acidulated water			
Carrots	1 lb	450 g	1 lb
Small turnips	1 lb	450 g	1 lb
Olive oil	3 tbsp	3 tbsp	3 tbsp
Large shallots, peeled	8	8	8
Vegetable stock	$\frac{1}{2}$ pt	300 ml	1$\frac{1}{4}$ cups
Bay leaves	2	2	2
Full fat soft cheese with herbs and garlic	150 g	5 oz	$\frac{2}{3}$ cup

Peel the celeriac, cut into large chunks and put immediately into the acidulated water. Peel the carrots and turnips and cut into similar sized chunks. Over a fairly high heat, heat the oil in the open pressure cooker and cook the vegetables, turning them over, for 1–2 minutes. Add the stock and bay leaves. Bring to pressure and cook for given time. Reduce pressure.

Transfer the vegetables to a warmed serving dish and keep warm. Remove and discard the bay leaves. Over a low heat, whisk the cheese into the stock. Pour over the vegetables.

COOKING TIME High/15-lb pressure 2$\frac{1}{2}$ minutes
Reduce pressure quickly

SERVES 4

Above: Triple Layered Gratin. Below: Quick Vegetable Ragout.

POTAGE DARBLAY

INGREDIENTS	IMPERIAL	METRIC	AMERICAN
Butter	2 oz	50 g	$\frac{1}{4}$ cup
Potatoes, thinly sliced	1 lb	450 g	1 lb
Onion, thinly sliced	1	1	1
Water	$\frac{3}{4}$ pt	400 ml	2 cups
Bay leaf	1	1	1
Salt and pepper			
Milk	$\frac{3}{4}$ pt	400 ml	2 cups
To garnish: Carrot, cut in thin strips	1	1	1
Celery stick, cut in thin strips	1	1	1
Onion, thinly sliced	1	1	1

Heat the butter in the open pressure cooker and gently sauté the potatoes and onion for 2–3 minutes. Add the water and bay leaf and season well.

Arrange the vegetables to be used as garnish in a separator and sit this on top of the soup. Bring to pressure and cook for given time. Reduce pressure.

Remove separator containing the vegetables and set it to one side. Discard the bay leaf. Purée the soup and return it to the pressure cooker. Stir in the milk, check the seasoning and reheat. Garnish with the cooked vegetables and serve.

COOKING TIME High/15-lb pressure 8 minutes
Reduce pressure slowly

SERVES 6

CELERY SOUP

INGREDIENTS	IMPERIAL	METRIC	AMERICAN
Butter	1 oz	25 g	2 tbsp
Large head celery, sliced	1	1	1
Onion, chopped	1	1	1
Water	$1\frac{3}{4}$ pt	1 l	4 cups
Salt and pepper			
Bouquet garni	1	1	1
Milk	$\frac{1}{2}$ pt	300 ml	$1\frac{1}{4}$ cups

Heat the butter in the open pressure cooker and sauté the celery and onion gently for 2–3 minutes. Add the water, seasoning and bouquet garni. Bring to pressure and cook for given time. Reduce pressure. Remove the bouquet garni. Purée the soup and return it to the pressure cooker. Reheat it and stir in the milk just before serving.

COOKING TIME High/15-lb pressure 10 minutes
Reduce pressure slowly

SERVES 4–6

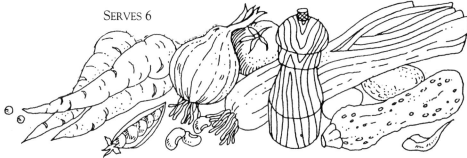

SAVOURY STARTERS

INGREDIENTS	IMPERIAL	METRIC	AMERICAN
Butter	1 tbsp	1 tbsp	1 tbsp
Small onion, chopped	1	1	1
Tomato, skinned and chopped	1	1	1
Made mustard	1 tsp	1 tsp	1 tsp
Salt and pepper			
Eggs	4	4	4
Milk	4 tbsp	4 tbsp	4 tbsp
Mushrooms, chopped	4	4	4
Toasted breadcrumbs			

Butter four individual ovenproof dishes. Mix together the onion, tomato and mustard, seasoning well with salt and pepper. Divide the mixture among the four dishes. Beat together the eggs, milk and mushrooms. Season and pour into each dish. Cover the dishes with foil, making sure the covers are tightly secured. Pour $\frac{1}{2}$ pt/300 ml/1$\frac{1}{4}$ cups water into the pressure cooker, position the trivet and place the dishes on it. Bring to pressure and cook for given time. Reduce pressure.

Sprinkle with toasted breadcrumbs and serve immediately.

COOKING TIME High/15-lb pressure 3 minutes
Reduce pressure slowly

CHECKPOINT Make sure the dishes do not touch the sides of the pressure cooker; they could crack. If necessary, stand three in a triangle with the fourth centred on top. Alternatively, cook them in two batches – it takes only a few minutes extra.

SERVES 4

BUTTER BEAN PÂTÉ

INGREDIENTS	IMPERIAL	METRIC	AMERICAN
Dried butter/lima beans	8 oz	225 g	$\frac{1}{2}$ lb
Ground cumin	2 tsp	2 tsp	2 tsp
Olive oil	3 tbsp	3 tbsp	3 tbsp
Juice of 2 lemons			
Cloves garlic, crushed	2	2	2
Chopped fresh coriander	2 tbsp	2 tbsp	2 tbsp
Salt and pepper			
Coriander sprigs and black olives, to garnish			

Pour boiling water over the beans and leave to soak for 1 hour. Drain. Place the beans in the pressure cooker with 1 pt/550 ml/2$\frac{1}{2}$ cups water. Bring to pressure and cook for given time. Reduce pressure.

Drain the beans and purée with the cumin, oil, lemon juice, garlic and coriander. Season to taste. Transfer to a bowl, cover and chill. Garnish with fresh coriander and olives. Serve with hot pitta bread, or warm Granary or wholemeal bread.

COOKING TIME High/15-lb pressure 12 minutes
Reduce pressure slowly

SERVES 4

BEAN PEPPER POT

INGREDIENTS	IMPERIAL	METRIC	AMERICAN
Flageolet beans	4 oz	100 g	$\frac{1}{4}$ lb
Cannellini beans	4 oz	100 g	$\frac{1}{4}$ lb
Red kidney beans	4 oz	100 g	$\frac{1}{4}$ lb
Cooking oil	2 tbsp	2 tbsp	2 tbsp
Onion, chopped	1	1	1
Cloves garlic, crushed	2	2	2
Celery sticks, sliced	2	2	2
Carrot, finely chopped	1	1	1
Red pepper, de-seeded and sliced	1	1	1
Paprika pepper	1 tbsp	1 tbsp	1 tbsp
Can tomatoes	14 oz	397 g	1 lb
Tomato purée/paste	4 tbsp	4 tbsp	4 tbsp
Fresh breadcrumbs	4 tbsp	4 tbsp	4 tbsp
Salt and pepper			
Chopped fresh parsley	2 tbsp	2 tbsp	2 tbsp
Soured cream (optional)	$\frac{1}{4}$ pt	150 ml	$\frac{2}{3}$ cup

Pour boiling water over the beans and leave to soak for 1 hour. Drain well. Heat the oil in the open pressure cooker and gently fry the onion, garlic and celery, stirring occasionally, until softened but not coloured. Stir in the carrot and red pepper and cook for about 2 minutes. Stir in the paprika and cook, stirring, for 2 minutes. Stir in the beans. Drain the juice from the tomatoes, blend with the tomato purée then make up to 3 pt/1.7 l/7$\frac{1}{2}$ cups with water. Add the tomatoes and liquid to the cooker.

Bring to the boil in the open cooker, skim any scum from the surface, adjust the heat so the contents are boiling gently but not rising. Bring to pressure over the same heat and cook for given time. Reduce pressure.

Stir in the breadcrumbs and boil to evaporate off surplus water and thicken the liquid. Adjust the seasoning and flavourings. Transfer to a warmed serving dish, stir in the parsley and swirl in the soured cream, if used.

COOKING TIME High/15-lb pressure 12 minutes
Reduce pressure slowly

SERVES 4

Left: Bean Pepper Pot. Right: Spicy Stuffed Onions.

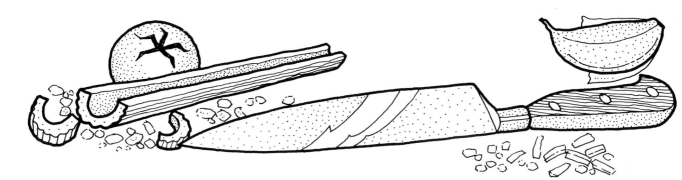

SPICY STUFFED ONIONS

INGREDIENTS	IMPERIAL	METRIC	AMERICAN
Large onions, peeled	4	4	4
Fresh breadcrumbs	4 oz	100 g	2 cups
Chopped mushrooms	4 tbsp	4 tbsp	4 tbsp
Chutney	2 tbsp	2 tbsp	2 tbsp
Curry powder	3 tsp	3 tsp	3 tsp
Worcestershire sauce	4 tsp	4 tsp	4 tsp
Salt			
Black pepper			

Sprigs of parsley, to
garnish

Using a teaspoon, scoop the centre out of each onion. Take a thin slice off the base of each with a sharp knife, so they will stand. In a bowl, mix together the remaining ingredients. Stuff each onion with the mixture. Pour $\frac{1}{2}$ pt/300 ml/$1\frac{1}{4}$ cups water into the pressure cooker and position the trivet. Stand the onions on the trivet. Bring to pressure and cook for given time. Reduce pressure. Garnish the onions with sprigs of parsley and serve.

COOKING TIME High/15-lb pressure 8 minutes
Reduce pressure quickly

SERVES 4

VEGETABLE HOTPOT

INGREDIENTS	IMPERIAL	METRIC	AMERICAN
Dried butter/lima beans	4 oz	100 g	$\frac{1}{4}$ lb
Butter	1 oz	25 g	2 tbsp
Large onion, sliced	1	1	1
Carrots, sliced	8 oz	225 g	$\frac{1}{2}$ lb
Dried mixed herbs	$\frac{1}{2}$ tsp	$\frac{1}{2}$ tsp	$\frac{1}{2}$ tsp
Stock			
Salt and pepper			
Short macaroni	4 oz	100 g	$\frac{1}{4}$ lb
Frozen peas	4 oz	100 g	$\frac{1}{4}$ lb
Croûtes: Butter, softened	1 oz	25 g	2 tbsp
Cheddar cheese, grated	2 oz	50 g	$\frac{1}{2}$ cup
Made mustard	1 tsp	1 tsp	1 tsp
Thick slices French bread	4	4	4

Place the butter beans in a large dish and cover with plenty of boiling water. Cover with a plate and leave for 1 hour. Heat the butter in the open pressure cooker and gently sauté the onion, carrots and herbs for 3–4 minutes. Drain the butter beans and add these to the pressure cooker. Make up the soaking liquid from the beans to 1 pt/550 ml/2 $\frac{1}{2}$ cups with stock. Add this to the bean mixture and season with salt and pepper. Bring to pressure and cook for given time. Reduce pressure.

Add the macaroni and peas to the vegetables, bring to pressure again and cook for given time. Reduce pressure. Pour the vegetables into a flameproof casserole.

Beat together the softened butter, cheese and mustard and spread on to one side of the bread slices. Place the bread, butter side up, on top of the casserole. Place under a hot grill/broiler until the cheese melts. Serve more cheese separately.

COOKING TIME High/15-lb pressure 15 minutes
Reduce pressure slowly
    macaroni added 5 minutes
Reduce pressure slowly

SERVES 4

POTATO PIE

INGREDIENTS	IMPERIAL	METRIC	AMERICAN
Butter			
Potatoes, peeled and sliced thinly	1 $\frac{1}{2}$ lb	700 g	1 $\frac{1}{2}$ lb
Onions, chopped	2	2	2
Grated nutmeg			
Salt and pepper			
Vegetable stock	$\frac{1}{4}$ pt	150 ml	$\frac{2}{3}$ cup
Cheese, grated	2 oz	50 g	$\frac{1}{2}$ cup

Butter an ovenproof dish which will fit into the pressure cooker. Layer the potatoes and onions in the dish. Sprinkle each layer with a little grated nutmeg and season well with salt and pepper. Pour the vegetable stock over the potatoes.

Pour $\frac{1}{2}$ pt/300 ml/1 $\frac{1}{4}$ cups water into pressure cooker and place the trivet in position. Stand the dish on the trivet, bring to pressure and cook for given time. Reduce pressure. Sprinkle the cheese over the potatoes and brown them under the grill/broiler before serving.

COOKING TIME High/15-lb pressure 13 minutes
Reduce pressure quickly

NOTE New potatoes might need slightly longer cooking times than those given.

This dish is also delicious made with garlic (omitting the nutmeg) and using canned tomatoes instead of the vegetable stock.

SERVES 4

POTATO LAYER

INGREDIENTS	IMPERIAL	METRIC	AMERICAN
Leeks, white part only, thinly sliced	8 oz	225 g	$\frac{1}{2}$ lb
Potatoes, peeled and very thinly sliced	$1\frac{1}{4}$ lb	550 g	$1\frac{1}{4}$ lb
Goats' cheese, crumbled	4 oz	100 g	$\frac{1}{4}$ lb
Salt and pepper			
Chopped fresh thyme			
Milk	15 fl oz	425 ml	scant 2 cups
Dry roasted peanuts, chopped	$1\frac{1}{2}$ oz	40 g	$\frac{1}{2}$ cup

Place the trivet in the pressure cooker and put the leeks on the trivet. Bring to pressure and cook for given time. Reduce pressure.

Place a layer of potato slices in the bottom of a buttered ovenproof dish. Cover with a layer of leeks then a layer of cheese, sprinkling freshly ground black pepper, chopped thyme and a very little salt over the potatoes and leeks. Continue layering, finishing with a layer of neatly overlapping potato slices followed by a layer of cheese. Pour over the milk. Cover the dish with foil or a double thickness of greaseproof/waxed paper and tie securely in place. Place the trivet in the cooker. Stand the dish on the trivet. Bring to pressure and cook for given time. Reduce pressure.

Remove the covering and sprinkle the nuts over the top to give a good, even covering. Place under a hot grill/broiler until lightly toasted.

COOKING TIME High/15-lb pressure leeks 1 minute
Reduce pressure quickly
  complete dish 25 minutes
Reduce pressure slowly

NOTE Feta cheese can be used in place of goats' cheese, or a well-flavoured Wensleydale or Cheddar (grated, not crumbled).

SERVES 4

TAGLIATELLI WITH ARTICHOKE SAUCE

INGREDIENTS	IMPERIAL	METRIC	AMERICAN
Squeeze of lemon juice			
Vegetable stock	$\frac{1}{2}$ pt	300 ml	$1\frac{1}{4}$ cups
Jerusalem artichokes, peeled and cubed	$1\frac{1}{4}$ lb	550 ml	$1\frac{1}{4}$ lb
Hard-boiled eggs, quartered	4	4	4
Tagliatelli	12 oz	350 g	$\frac{3}{4}$ lb
Walnut or olive oil	2 tbsp	2 tbsp	2 tbsp
Unsalted butter, diced	25 g	1 oz	2 tbsp
Soured cream	6 fl oz	175 ml	$\frac{3}{4}$ cup
Salt and pepper			
Walnut halves, finely chopped	2 oz	50 g	$\frac{1}{2}$ cup

Add the lemon juice to the stock then pour into the pressure cooker. Peel the Jerusalem artichokes, cut into cubes and put immediately into the cooker. Bring to pressure and cook for given time.

Meanwhile, cut the quarters of egg in half. Line the separator basket with oiled foil, put in the tagliatelli. Reduce pressure. Place the basket over the artichokes, return to pressure and cook for given time. Reduce pressure.

Drain the tagliatelli, then toss with the oil and egg. Turn into a warmed dish, cover and keep warm. Purée the artichokes with the butter and soured cream. Warm through gently, stirring, in the open cooker, season to taste then spoon over the pasta. Scatter the nuts over the top and place under a hot grill/broiler until browned.

COOKING TIME High/15-lb pressure Jerusalem
  artichokes 2 minutes
  tagliatelli added $1\frac{1}{2}$ minutes
Reduce pressure slowly

SERVES 4

SAVOURY BROWN RICE

INGREDIENTS	IMPERIAL	METRIC	AMERICAN
Vegetable stock or water (optional)	3 pt	1.7 l	7½ cups
Brown rice	8 oz	225 g	generous 1 cup
Plain yogurt	4 tbsp	4 tbsp	4 tbsp
Lemon juice	1 tbsp	1 tbsp	1 tbsp
Olive oil	1 tbsp	1 tbsp	1 tbsp
Chopped fresh mixed herbs	2 tbsp	2 tbsp	2 tbsp
Wholegrain mustard	2 tbsp	2 tbsp	2 tbsp
Salt and pepper			
Button mushrooms, thinly sliced	8 oz	225 g	2 cups
Small, ripe avocado, peeled, chopped and tossed in lemon juice	1	1	1
Hazelnuts, chopped	4 oz	100 g	1 cup
Cooked peas or thawed frozen peas	2 oz	50 g	½ cup
Dried apricots, chopped	2 oz	50 g	⅓ cup
Watercress, to garnish			

Bring the stock or water to the boil in the open pressure cooker, add the rice, stir and return to the boil. Adjust the heat so the contents are just boiling but not rising in the cooker. Bring to pressure over the same heat and cook for given time.

Meanwhile, mix the yogurt, lemon juice, oil, herbs, mustard, salt and plenty of freshly ground black pepper together.

Reduce pressure. Strain the rice and return to the

Above: Savoury Brown Rice. Left: Spiced Cabbage. Right: Potato Mint Soup (page 12).

open cooker over a low heat, and fluff it up with a fork. Tip into a bowl and fork the dressing and remaining ingredients through the warm rice. Leave to cool completely. Cover then chill.

COOKING TIME High/15-lb pressure 3 minutes
Reduce pressure slowly

SERVES 4–6

SPICED CABBAGE

INGREDIENTS	IMPERIAL	METRIC	AMERICAN
Butter	2 oz	50 g	¼ cup
Small onion, chopped	1	1	1
Small red cabbage, shredded	1	1	1
Cooking apple, peeled, cored, chopped	1	1	1
Sultanas/white raisins	1 oz	25 g	2 tbsp
Wine vinegar	2 tbsp	2 tbsp	2 tbsp
Water	2 tbsp	2 tbsp	2 tbsp
Brown sugar	1 tbsp	1 tbsp	1 tbsp
Salt and pepper			

Heat the butter in the open pressure cooker and sauté the onion gently until transparent. Add the remaining ingredients, bring to pressure and cook for given time. Reduce pressure. Serve hot or cold with cold cooked meat.

COOKING TIME High/15-lb pressure 4 minutes
Reduce pressure quickly

NOTE This recipe probably does not include the minimum amount of liquid recommended by the manufacturer of your pressure cooker. It may, however, be successfully prepared where ¼–½ pt/ 150–300 ml/⅔–1¼ cups liquid is required.

SERVES 4

SAVOURY BREAD PUDDING

INGREDIENTS	IMPERIAL	METRIC	AMERICAN
Slices wholemeal or Granary bread	4	4	4
Peanut butter, tahini or butter, for spreading			
Tomatoes, skinned, de-seeded, chopped	3	3	3
Mature Cheddar cheese, grated	4 oz	100 g	1 cup
Milk, warmed	$\frac{1}{2}$ pt	300 ml	$1\frac{1}{4}$ cups
Soft cheese with herbs	4 oz	100 g	$\frac{1}{4}$ lb
Eggs, lightly beaten and strained	2	2	2
Black pepper			
Porridge oats	25 g	1 oz	2 tbsp

Spread the bread thinly with peanut butter. Remove the crusts.

Layer the bread, tomatoes and 75 g/3 oz/$\frac{3}{4}$ cup of the cheese in a buttered ovenproof dish. Beat the milk into the soft cheese, then beat in the eggs. Add the pepper and pour over the bread. Leave to soak for 20–30 minutes. Cover the dish with foil or a double thickness of greaseproof/waxed paper and secure tightly. Pour 1 pt/550 ml/$2\frac{1}{2}$ cups water into the pressure cooker and position the trivet. Place the dish on the trivet. Bring to pressure and cook for given time. Reduce pressure.

Mix the remaining grated cheese and the oats together and sprinkle over the top of the pudding. Place under a hot grill/broiler until golden. Leave the pudding to stand for a couple of minutes before serving.

COOKING TIME High/15-lb pressure 10 minutes
Reduce pressure slowly

SERVES 4

CAULIFLOWER WITH WALNUT SAUCE

INGREDIENTS	IMPERIAL	METRIC	AMERICAN
Vegetable stock	$\frac{1}{2}$ pt	300 ml	$1\frac{1}{4}$ cups
Cauliflower, divided into florets	1	1	1
Medium-bodied dry white wine (optional)	3 fl oz	75 ml	$\frac{1}{3}$ cup
Walnut halves	5 oz	150 g	$1\frac{1}{4}$ cups
Cloves garlic, crushed	1–2	1–2	1–2
Slice wholemeal or Granary bread, crusts removed, soaked in water	$\frac{1}{2}$ oz	15 g	$\frac{1}{2}$ oz
Juice of 1 lemon			
Ground mace	1 tsp	1 tsp	1 tsp
Salt and pepper			
Walnuts, chopped	2 oz	50 g	$\frac{1}{2}$ cup

Put the trivet into the pressure cooker, pour in the stock and put the cauliflower on the trivet. Bring to pressure and cook for given time. Reduce pressure.

Transfer the cauliflower to a warmed serving dish. Remove the trivet from the cooker, add the wine to the stock, if used, then boil until reduced to 6 fl oz/175 ml/$\frac{3}{4}$ cup.

Chop the walnut halves and garlic coarsely in a blender or food processor. Squeeze out the bread and add to the nuts with the reduced stock and lemon juice. Blend to a smooth, light sauce. Add mace and seasoning to taste. Toss the chopped walnuts with the cauliflower and pour the sauce over.

COOKING TIME High/15-lb pressure 2 minutes
Reduce pressure quickly

SERVES 4

ONION BUTTER BEANS

INGREDIENTS	IMPERIAL	METRIC	AMERICAN
Dried butter/lima beans	8 oz	225 g	$\frac{1}{2}$ lb
Butter	2 oz	50 g	$\frac{1}{4}$ cup
Large onions, chopped	2	2	2
Good pinch mace			
Salt and pepper			
Flour	3–4 tbsp	3–4 tbsp	3–4 tbsp
Milk	$\frac{1}{4}$ pt	150 ml	$\frac{2}{3}$ cup
Cheese, grated	4 oz	100 g	1 cup

Place the butter beans in a dish and cover with boiling water. Leave to soak for 1 hour. Heat the butter in the open pressure cooker and gently sauté the onions until transparent. Add the drained butter beans, mace and seasoning. Make the soaking liquid from the beans up to 1 pt/550 ml/2$\frac{1}{2}$ cups with water and stir into the bean mixture. Bring to pressure and cook for given time. Reduce pressure.

Mix the flour with a little of the milk to form a smooth paste and add it to the beans. Stir in the rest of the milk. Bring to the boil, stirring well. Pour the beans into an ovenproof serving dish and sprinkle them with the grated cheese. Brown under a hot grill/broiler before serving.

COOKING TIME High/15-lb pressure 20 minutes
Reduce pressure slowly

SERVES 4

SWEETCORN TIMBALE

INGREDIENTS	IMPERIAL	METRIC	AMERICAN
Sweetcorn kernels	10 oz	275 g	1$\frac{3}{4}$ cups
Milk	$\frac{1}{2}$ pt	300 ml	1$\frac{1}{4}$ cups
Eggs, beaten and strained	2	2	2
Unsalted butter, just melted	2 oz	50 g	$\frac{1}{4}$ cup
Finely chopped fresh parsley	2 tbsp	2 tbsp	2 tbsp
Salt and pepper			

Purée the sweetcorn kernels coarsely, then mix with the remaining ingredients. Pour into a 2 pt/1.1 l/5 cup heatproof bowl, cover with a lid, or foil or double thickness of greaseproof/waxed paper tied securely in place.

Put the trivet into the pressure cooker, pour in $\frac{3}{4}$ pt/400 ml/2 cups water then stand the bowl on the trivet. Bring to pressure and cook for given time. Reduce pressure. Leave the timbale to stand for a few minutes before serving.

COOKING TIME High/15-lb pressure 23 minutes
Reduce pressure slowly

SERVES 4

DESSERTS

Fruits, both fresh or dried, custards, milk puddings and sponge puddings are all ideal candidates for pressure-cooking. Enormous time and fuel savings are involved when pressure-cooking most desserts.

Fresh fruits can be quickly cooked or puréed in your pressure cooker. Dried fruits need only a few minutes soaking in boiling water before pressure-cooking and can therefore be used to make speedy desserts.

Unexpectedly, perhaps, egg custards cook perfectly in your pressure cooker without the usual temperature watching. An automatic timer is a 'must' though.

A great advantage when pressure-cooking steamed puddings is the lack of steam. In addition, there is no need for constant checking to see if there is sufficient water in the pan.

PEARS IN RED WINE

INGREDIENTS	IMPERIAL	METRIC	AMERICAN
Medium pears, peeled, halved and cored	6	6	6
Caster/superfine sugar	3 oz	75 g	6 tbsp
Juice $\frac{1}{2}$ lemon			
Redcurrant jelly	4 tbsp	4 tbsp	4 tbsp
Red wine	$\frac{3}{4}$ pt	400 ml	2 cups
Whipped cream, to decorate			

Arrange the pear halves in the pressure cooker without the trivet and sprinkle with the sugar and lemon juice. Add the redcurrant jelly and red wine. Bring to pressure and cook for given time. Reduce pressure.

Arrange the pears in a serving dish and pour the juice over and around them. Chill, decorate with whipped cream and serve.

COOKING TIME High/15-lb pressure 4–8 minutes
Reduce pressure quickly

SERVES 6

PEACH COMPOTE

INGREDIENTS	IMPERIAL	METRIC	AMERICAN
Peaches, peeled, halved and stoned/pitted	8	8	8
Red wine	$\frac{3}{4}$ pt	400 ml	2 cups
Grated rind and juice of 2 oranges			
Flaked almonds	2 tbsp	2 tbsp	2 tbsp
Sugar (optional)			

Arrange the peach halves in the pressure cooker and add the red wine, orange rind and juice and flaked almonds. If liked, sweeten with a little sugar. Bring to pressure and cook for given time. Reduce pressure.

Serve chilled with macaroons.

COOKING TIME High/15-lb pressure 4 minutes
Reduce pressure quickly

SERVES 8

Opposite: Pears in Red Wine.

DATE PUDDING

INGREDIENTS	IMPERIAL	METRIC	AMERICAN
Self-raising flour or plain flour sifted with 1 tsp baking powder	4 oz	100 g	1 cup
Mixed spice	$\frac{1}{2}$ tsp	$\frac{1}{2}$ tsp	$\frac{1}{2}$ tsp
Pinch salt			
Butter	3 oz	75 g	6 tbsp
Rounded tbsp breadcrumbs	4	4	4
Rounded tbsp brown sugar	2	2	2
Dates, chopped	4 oz	100 g	$\frac{1}{4}$ lb
Eggs, beaten	2	2	2
Golden/corn syrup	1 tbsp	1 tbsp	1 tbsp
Milk, to mix			

Butter a $1\frac{1}{2}$-pt/1-l/4-cup pudding basin.

Sieve together the flour, spice and salt. Rub in the butter then stir in the breadcrumbs, sugar and dates. Mix together the eggs and syrup and add them to the dry ingredients. Mix well, adding a little milk if necessary to make a smooth dropping consistency. Put the mixture into the prepared basin and cover securely with foil or a double layer of greaseproof/waxed paper.

Pour $1\frac{1}{2}$ pt/1 l/4 cups water into the pressure cooker and position the trivet. Stand the pudding on the trivet. Pre-steam the pudding (see page 100), then bring to pressure and cook for given time. Reduce pressure. Serve with custard.

COOKING TIME Pre-steaming 25 minutes
Low/5-lb pressure 25 minutes
Reduce pressure slowly

SERVES 4

QUICK-BAKED APPLES

INGREDIENTS	IMPERIAL	METRIC	AMERICAN
Soft brown sugar	2 oz	50 g	$\frac{1}{4}$ cup
Ground cinnamon	$\frac{1}{2}$ tsp	$\frac{1}{2}$ tsp	$\frac{1}{2}$ tsp
Pinch ground cloves			
Sultanas/white raisins	4 oz	100 g	$\frac{2}{3}$ cup
Juice $\frac{1}{2}$ lemon			
Medium cooking apples, cored	4	4	4

Mix together the sugar, cinnamon, cloves, sultanas and lemon juice. Pack the core hollows of the apples tightly with the mixture. Pour $\frac{1}{2}$ pt/300 ml/$1\frac{1}{4}$ cups water into the pressure cooker and position the trivet. Stand the apples on top, bring to pressure and cook for given time. Reduce pressure.

Arrange the apples on a serving dish and serve with cream or custard.

COOKING TIME High/15-lb pressure 4 minutes
Reduce pressure slowly

SERVES 4

FRUIT HAT

INGREDIENTS	IMPERIAL	METRIC	AMERICAN
Self-raising flour or plain flour sifted with 1 tsp baking powder	4 oz	100 g	1 cup
Pinch salt			
Butter, melted	6 oz	175 g	$\frac{3}{4}$ cup
Fresh white breadcrumbs	4 oz	100 g	2 cups
Large egg, beaten	1	1	1
Milk, to mix			
Stewed or canned fruit such as blackcurrants, plums, cherries	1 lb	450 g	1 lb
Sugar			

Butter a $1\frac{1}{2}$-pt/1-l/4-cup pudding basin.

Sieve together the flour and salt and mix in the melted butter. Stir in the breadcrumbs and mix to a stiff dough with the beaten egg and a little milk. Roll two-thirds of the dough into a circle and use it to line the prepared basin. Put the strained fruit (sweetened to taste) into the pudding and dampen the edges of the dough. Roll the remaining dough into a circle and place it on top of the pudding, sealing the edges before trimming. Cover securely with foil or a double layer of buttered greaseproof/waxed paper.

Pour $1\frac{1}{2}$ pt/1 l/4 cups water into the pressure cooker and position the trivet. Stand the pudding on top. Pre-steam the pudding (see page 100) then bring to pressure and cook for given time. Reduce pressure.

Turn out the pudding. The juice from the strained fruit may be thickened with a little cornflour/cornstarch to make an accompanying sauce.

COOKING TIME Pre-steaming 15 minutes
Low/5-lb pressure 40 minutes
Reduce pressure slowly

SERVES 4

APRICOT CONDÉ

INGREDIENTS	IMPERIAL	METRIC	AMERICAN
Quantity Vanilla Rice Pudding (see page 93)	1	1	1
Single/thin cream	2 tbsp	2 tbsp	2 tbsp
Cooked dried apricots			

Cook the rice pudding as indicated in the recipe and allow it to cool. Mix the cold rice pudding with a little cream and some drained chopped apricots. Spoon it into individual dishes and decorate with more fruit.

NOTE This may be served with cooked fresh or canned fruit.

SERVES 4

89

MULLED WINTER FRUIT COMPÔTE

INGREDIENTS	IMPERIAL	METRIC	AMERICAN
Mixed dried fruits, stoned/pitted, e.g. prunes, apricots, pears, peaches, figs	8 oz	225 g	$\frac{1}{2}$ lb
Oranges	2	2	2
Long strip of lemon rind			
Cinnamon stick, halved	1 inch	2.5 cm	1 inch
Cloves	2	2	2
Sweet sherry	$\frac{1}{4}$ pt	150 ml	$\frac{2}{3}$ cup
Sweet white wine	$\frac{1}{4}$ pt	150 ml	$\frac{2}{3}$ cup
Toasted flaked almonds	2 tbsp	2 tbsp	2 tbsp
Whipped cream, fromage blanc or strained Greek yogurt, to serve			

Put the dried fruits into a bowl. Grate the rind and squeeze the juice from 1 of the oranges. Add to the bowl with the lemon rind and spices. Heat the sherry and wine to just below simmering point and pour into the bowl. Cover and leave to soak for 10 minutes.

Pour the contents of the bowl into the pressure cooker. Bring to pressure and cook for 6–8 minutes, depending how soft you like the fruit to be.

Meanwhile, peel the remaining orange and divide into segments. Reduce pressure. Remove the cinnamon stick and serve the compote warm with the orange segments and flaked almonds scattered over. Accompany with whipped cream, fromage blanc or strained Greek yogurt.

COOKING TIME High/15-lb pressure 6–8 minutes
Reduce pressure slowly

SERVES 4

ROSE CREAMS

INGREDIENTS	IMPERIAL	METRIC	AMERICAN
Whipping or double cream	18 fl oz	500 ml	$2\frac{1}{4}$ cups
Egg yolks	4	4	4
Caster/superfine sugar	2 oz	50 g	$\frac{1}{4}$ cup
Rose water	1–2 tbsp	1–2 tbsp	1–2 tbsp
Raspberries, fresh or frozen, thawed	12 oz	350 g	$\frac{3}{4}$ lb
Crystallized or fresh rose petals, for decoration			
Crisp biscuits/cookies, such as tuile d'amandes, to serve			

Heat the cream to just below simmering point, then strain on to the egg yolks, stirring. Stir in the sugar and rose water, to taste. Pour into four buttered, individual, ovenproof dishes. Cover the dishes with foil or a double thickness of greaseproof/waxed paper and tie tightly in place. Pour $\frac{1}{2}$ pt/300 ml/1$\frac{1}{4}$ cups water into the pressure cooker, put the trivet in place and stand the dishes on the trivet. Bring to pressure and cook for given time. Reduce pressure.

Remove the dishes and uncover them. Leave to cool, then chill lightly. Purée the raspberries and pass through a non-metallic sieve. Unmould the rose creams, pour the sauce around and decorate with crystallized or fresh rose petals. Serve with crisp biscuits.

COOKING TIME High/15-lb pressure 4 minutes
Reduce pressure slowly

SERVES 4

Left: Rose Creams. Right: Mulled Winter Fruit Compôte.

EGG CUSTARD

INGREDIENTS	IMPERIAL	METRIC	AMERICAN
Eggs, beaten	3	3	3
Caster/superfine sugar	2 oz	50 g	$\frac{1}{4}$ cup
Few drops almond essence			
Milk	1 pt	550 ml	$2\frac{1}{2}$ cups
Grated nutmeg			

Mix together the eggs, sugar and almond essence. Warm the milk and blend with the eggs. Pour the mixture into a buttered $1\frac{1}{2}$-pt/1-l/4-cup basin. Sprinkle with a little grated nutmeg and cover securely with foil or a double layer of greaseproof/waxed paper.

Pour 1 pt/550 ml/$2\frac{1}{2}$ cups water into the pressure cooker. Position the trivet and stand the basin on top. Bring to pressure and cook for given time. Reduce pressure.

COOKING TIME High/15-lb pressure 10 minutes
Reduce pressure slowly

NOTE Other flavourings may be used to replace the almond essence. Try vanilla essence or a few teaspoons of instant coffee, dissolved in a little cold water.

SERVES 4

CRÈME CARAMEL

INGREDIENTS	IMPERIAL	METRIC	AMERICAN
Caramel: Sugar	4 oz	100 g	$\frac{1}{2}$ cup
Water	$\frac{1}{4}$ pt	150 ml	$\frac{2}{3}$ cup
Custard: Eggs, beaten	3	3	3
Sugar	1 oz	25 g	2 tbsp
Few drops vanilla essence			
Milk	$\frac{3}{4}$ pt	400 ml	2 cups

To make the caramel: put the sugar and water into a small saucepan and dissolve the sugar slowly over a low heat. Bring to the boil until it caramelizes (turns a golden brown). Pour the caramel into four warmed cups or bowls. Allow to cool.

Mix together the eggs, sugar and vanilla essence. Warm the milk and pour it on to the eggs. Strain this mixture and pour it over the cooled caramel. Cover the cups or bowls securely with foil or a double layer of greaseproof/waxed paper.

Pour $\frac{1}{2}$ pt/300 ml/$1\frac{1}{4}$ cups water into the pressure cooker, position the trivet and stand the cups or bowls on top.

Bring to pressure and cook for given time. Reduce pressure. Chill for several hours before serving. To serve, ease the edge of the custard away from the dish and turn it out.

COOKING TIME High/15-lb pressure 3 minutes
Reduce pressure slowly

NOTE The shape and size of the dishes used will determine exact cooking times. You will probably need to experiment with your own dishes to find the correct time. Crème Caramel is easier to turn out if really cold.

SERVES 4

BANANA AND PRUNE BAKE

INGREDIENTS	IMPERIAL	METRIC	AMERICAN
Dried prunes	8 oz	225 g	$\frac{1}{2}$ lb
Sugar	2 oz	50 g	$\frac{1}{4}$ cup
Concentrated orange juice	6 fl oz	175 ml	$\frac{3}{4}$ cup
Arrowroot	2 tbsp	2 tbsp	2 tbsp
Bananas	2	2	2
Juice 1 lemon			
Butter	1 oz	25 g	2 tbsp

Place the prunes in a bowl and cover them with boiling water. Cover with a plate and leave for 1 hour. Drain the prunes, reserving the liquid, arrange them in the pressure cooker without the trivet and sprinkle with sugar. Make up the soaking liquid from the prunes to $\frac{1}{2}$ pt/300 ml/1$\frac{1}{4}$ cups with water and mix with the concentrated orange juice. Add the orange mixture to the prunes, bring to pressure and cook for given time. Reduce pressure.

Using a draining spoon lift out the prunes and arrange them in four small flameproof dishes. Mix the arrowroot with a little cold water to form a smooth paste and stir into the sauce. Bring to the boil, stirring continuously. Pour some of the sauce into each dish of prunes, leaving about $\frac{1}{2}$ inch/1 cm headspace.

Slice the bananas and toss them gently in the lemon juice. Arrange the banana slices on top of the prunes, dot them with butter and brown under a hot grill/broiler. Serve immediately.

COOKING TIME High/15-lb pressure 10 minutes
Reduce pressure slowly

SERVES 4

VANILLA RICE PUDDING

INGREDIENTS	IMPERIAL	METRIC	AMERICAN
Butter	1 oz	25 g	2 tbsp
Milk	1 pt	550 ml	2$\frac{1}{2}$ cups
Pudding rice	2 oz	50 g	$\frac{1}{3}$ cup
Sugar	2 oz	50 g	$\frac{1}{4}$ cup
Vanilla essence	1 tsp	1 tsp	1 tsp
Good pinch grated nutmeg			

Melt the butter in the open pressure cooker without the trivet and pour in the milk. Bring to the boil and add the remaining ingredients. Bring to the boil again, then lower the heat so that the milk simmers gently. Bring to pressure on this heat and cook for given time. Reduce pressure.

Stir the pudding and pour it into a warmed serving dish. If liked, brown it under a hot grill/broiler before serving.

COOKING TIME High/15-lb pressure 12 minutes
Reduce pressure slowly

NOTE Try using cinnamon or mixed spice to replace the vanilla and nutmeg.

SERVES 4

CHOCOLATE PUDDING

INGREDIENTS	IMPERIAL	METRIC	AMERICAN
Margarine	4 oz	100 g	$\frac{1}{2}$ cup
Caster/superfine sugar	4 oz	100 g	$\frac{1}{2}$ cup
Large eggs, beaten	2	2	2
Self-raising flour or plain flour sifted with $1\frac{1}{2}$ tsp baking powder	6 oz	150 g	$1\frac{1}{2}$ cups
Cocoa powder	2 tsp	2 tsp	2 tsp
Chopped plain/ semi-sweet chocolate	4 oz	100 g	$\frac{1}{2}$ cup
Milk, to mix			

Butter a 1-pt/550-ml/$2\frac{1}{2}$-cup pudding basin. Cream the margarine and sugar until light and fluffy, and gradually beat in the egg. Sieve together the flour and cocoa powder and fold them gently into the mixture along with the chopped chocolate. Add a little milk if necessary to make a smooth dropping consistency. Put the mixture into the prepared basin and cover it securely with foil or a double layer of buttered greaseproof/waxed paper.

Pour $1\frac{1}{2}$ pt/1 1/4 cups water into the pressure cooker. Position the trivet and stand the pudding on top. Pre-steam the pudding (see page 100) then bring to pressure and cook for given time. Reduce pressure. Serve with custard or sweet white sauce.

COOKING TIME Pre-steaming 25 minutes
Low/5-lb pressure 25 minutes
Reduce pressure slowly

SERVES 4

RASPBERRY CREAM

INGREDIENTS	IMPERIAL	METRIC	AMERICAN
Quantity Egg Custard recipe (see page 92)	1	1	1
Can raspberries	1 med	1 med	1 med
Cornflour/cornstarch	1 tbsp	1 tbsp	1 tbsp
Double/thick cream	$\frac{1}{4}$ pt	150 ml	$\frac{2}{3}$ cup
Chopped nuts, to decorate			

Prepare the egg custard, omitting the nutmeg, then cool it slightly. Drain the raspberries and arrange them in a serving bowl. Mix the cornflour with the raspberry juice and bring to the boil, stirring well. Pour this juice over the raspberries and allow it to cool. Stir the cream into the egg custard and pour it over the raspberry mixture. Chill before serving and decorate with chopped nuts.

SERVES 4–6

Crème Brûlée

Ingredients	Imperial	Metric	American
Single/thin cream	$\frac{1}{2}$ pt	300 ml	$1\frac{1}{4}$ cups
Double/thick cream	$\frac{1}{2}$ pt	300 ml	$1\frac{1}{4}$ cups
Egg yolks	4	4	4
Vanilla essence	1 tsp	1 tsp	1 tsp
Caster/superfine sugar	4–5 tbsp	4–5 tbsp	4–5 tbsp

Butter an ovenproof serving dish. Heat the single and double creams together in a saucepan (but do not allow to boil). Mix together the egg yolks, vanilla essence and 1 tbsp of the sugar, and pour the warmed cream over the eggs. Pour the mixture into the prepared dish and cover it securely with foil.

Pour $\frac{1}{2}$ pt/300 ml/$1\frac{1}{4}$ cups water into the pressure cooker with the trivet. Stand the dish on the trivet. Bring to pressure and cook for given time. Reduce pressure.

Chill the cream for several hours or preferably overnight. Pre-heat the grill/broiler. Dust the top of the cream evenly with the remaining sugar and place it under the grill (at least 4 inches/10 cm away) so the sugar melts and begins to brown. Chill for 2–3 hours before serving. This rich dessert is delicious served with sugared fresh fruit:

Cooking Time High/15-lb pressure 5 minutes
Reduce pressure slowly

SERVES 4

Spiced Fruit Pudding

Ingredients	Imperial	Metric	American
Self-raising flour or plain flour sifted with 1 tsp baking powder	4 oz	100 g	1 cup
Pinch salt			
Ground cinnamon	2 tsp	2 tsp	2 tsp
Grated nutmeg	2 tsp	2 tsp	2 tsp
Butter	3 oz	75 g	6 tbsp
Caster/superfine sugar	3 oz	75 g	6 tbsp
Fresh brown breadcrumbs	4 oz	100 g	2 cups
Mixed dried fruit	4 oz	100 g	$\frac{2}{3}$ cup
Egg, beaten	1	1	1
Milk, to mix			

Butter a $1\frac{1}{2}$-pt/1-l/4-cup pudding basin.

Sieve together the flour, salt, cinnamon and 1 tsp of the nutmeg, then rub in the butter until the mixture resembles fine breadcrumbs. Stir in the sugar, breadcrumbs, fruit and remaining nutmeg. Mix in the beaten egg, adding a little milk if necessary to make a smooth dropping consistency. Put the mixture into the prepared basin and cover securely with foil or a double layer of buttered greaseproof/waxed paper. Pour $1\frac{1}{2}$ pt/1 l/4 cups water into the pressure cooker, position the trivet and stand the basin on top. Pre-steam the pudding (see page 100), then bring to pressure and cook for given time. Reduce pressure. Serve with cream or custard.

Cooking Time Pre-steaming 25 minutes
High/15-lb pressure 45 minutes
Reduce pressure slowly

SERVES 4

FRUITY PUDDING

INGREDIENTS	IMPERIAL	METRIC	AMERICAN
Apricot jam	2 tbsp	2 tbsp	2 tbsp
Margarine	3 oz	75 g	6 tbsp
Caster/superfine sugar	3 oz	75 g	6 tbsp
Grated rind 1 lemon			
Large egg, beaten	1	1	1
Self-raising flour or plain flour with 1½ tsp baking powder	6 oz	150 g	1½ cups
Milk, to mix			

Butter a 1-pt/550-ml/2½-cup pudding basin and put the jam in the base. Cream together the margarine, sugar and lemon rind until light and fluffy. Gradually beat in the egg, then fold in the sieved flour. Add a little milk if necessary to make a smooth dropping consistency. Put the mixture into the prepared basin and cover it securely with foil or a double layer of buttered greaseproof/waxed paper.

Pour 1½ pt/1 1/4 cups water into the pressure cooker. Position the trivet and stand the basin on top. Pre-steam the pudding (see page 100) then bring to pressure and cook for given time. Reduce pressure. Serve with custard.

COOKING TIME Pre-steaming 15 minutes
Low/5-lb pressure 25 minutes
Reduce pressure slowly

SERVES 4

PEACHES IN VANILLA SAUCE

INGREDIENTS	IMPERIAL	METRIC	AMERICAN
Medium peaches	4	4	4
Sugar	1 oz	25 g	2 tbsp
Vanilla essence	1 tsp	1 tsp	1 tsp
Water	¼ pt	150 ml	⅔ cup
Dry cider or white wine	¼ pt	150 ml	⅔ cup
Cornflour/cornstarch	1 tbsp	1 tbsp	1 tbsp
Single/thin cream	¼ pt	150 ml	⅔ cup

Skin the peaches by plunging them into boiling water for 1–2 minutes. Halve and stone them. Arrange the peaches in the pressure cooker without the trivet and sprinkle them with the sugar. Add vanilla essence, water and cider or wine. Bring to pressure and cook for given time. Reduce pressure.

Arrange the peach halves on a serving dish. Mix the cornflour with a little cold water to form a smooth paste and add it to the liquor in the pressure cooker. Bring to the boil, stirring well. Just before serving, stir the cream into the hot (not boiling) sauce and pour it over the peaches.

COOKING TIME High/15-lb pressure 4 minutes
Reduce pressure quickly

SERVES 4

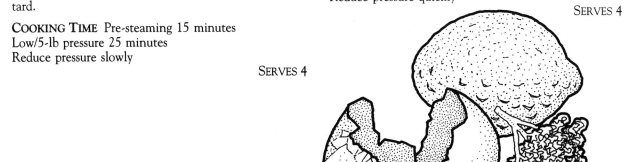

CHRISTMAS PUDDING

INGREDIENTS	IMPERIAL	METRIC	AMERICAN
Self-raising flour or plain flour sifted with $\frac{1}{2}$-tsp baking powder	2 oz	50 g	$\frac{1}{2}$ cup
Pinch salt			
Each of, grated nutmeg, mixed spice, cinnamon	$\frac{1}{2}$ tsp	$\frac{1}{2}$ tsp	$\frac{1}{2}$ tsp
Fresh white breadcrumbs	3 oz	75 g	$1\frac{1}{2}$ cups
Beef suet, shredded or finely chopped	3 oz	75 g	$\frac{2}{3}$ cup
Demerara/brown sugar	2 oz	50 g	$\frac{1}{4}$ cup
Each, currants, raisins, sultanas/white raisins, mixed peel	4 oz	100 g	$\frac{2}{3}$ cup
Chopped almonds	1 oz	25 g	$\frac{1}{4}$ cup
Eggs, beaten	2	2	2
Grated rind and juice of 1 orange			
Brandy	2 tbsp	2 tbsp	2 tbsp
Milk, ale or stout, to mix			

Butter two 1-pt/550 ml/2$\frac{1}{2}$-cup pudding basins. Sieve the flour with the salt and spices. Add all dry ingredients and mix well. Mix together the beaten eggs, orange rind and juice, brandy and a little milk. Add these to the fruit mixture and stir well. Turn into the prepared basins and cover securely with foil or a double layer of buttered greaseproof/waxed paper. Pour 2$\frac{1}{2}$ pt/1.5 l/6$\frac{1}{4}$ cups water into the pressure cooker and position the trivet. Stand the puddings on the trivet. Pre-steam the puddings for the time shown then bring to pressure and cook for given time. Reduce pressure. Serve with brandy sauce.

COOKING TIME Pre-steaming 20 minutes
High/15-lb pressure 1$\frac{3}{4}$ hours
Reduce pressure slowly

REHEATING TIME High/15-lb pressure 20 minutes
Reduce pressure slowly

CHECKPOINT The puddings should be prepared in October so that they have time to mature before Christmas. If your pressure cooker is large enough, cook the puddings side by side on the trivet, or one on top of the other with the trivet between. The basins must not touch the sides or the lid.

MAKES 2 × 1 lb/450 g puddings

APPLE AND DATE DESSERT

INGREDIENTS	IMPERIAL	METRIC	AMERICAN
Cooking apples, peeled, cored and sliced	1 lb	450 g	1 lb
Demerara/brown sugar	2 oz	50 g	$\frac{1}{4}$ cup
Dates, chopped	2 oz	50 g	$\frac{1}{4}$ cup
Water	2 tbsp	2 tbsp	2 tbsp
Double/thick cream	$\frac{1}{4}$ pt	150 ml	$\frac{2}{3}$ cup
Chopped walnuts, to decorate			

Arrange the apple slices in an ovenproof dish and sprinkle them with the sugar, chopped dates and water. Cover securely with foil. Pour $\frac{1}{2}$ pt/300 ml/1$\frac{1}{4}$ cups water into the pressure cooker. Position the trivet and stand the dish on top. Bring to pressure and cook for given time. Reduce pressure.

Mash the apple mixture with a fork and stir in the cream. Serve hot or cold in individual dishes and decorate with chopped walnuts.

COOKING TIME Medium/10-lb pressure 1 minute
Reduce pressure slowly

SERVES 4

BREAD AND BUTTER PUDDING

INGREDIENTS	IMPERIAL	METRIC	AMERICAN
Sliced buttered bread, cut into triangles	4–6	4–6	4–6
Sultanas/white raisins	2 oz	50 g	$\frac{1}{3}$ cup
Currants	2 oz	50 g	$\frac{1}{3}$ cup
Caster/superfine sugar	1 oz	25 g	2 tbsp
Milk	$\frac{3}{4}$ pt	400 ml	2 cups
Large eggs, beaten	2	2	2
Grated nutmeg			

Butter a suitable ovenproof dish and layer the bread triangles in the dish with the sultanas, currants and sugar. Warm the milk and pour on to the beaten eggs, stirring well. Pour this mixture over the bread and sprinkle it with grated nutmeg. Cover the basin securely with foil or a double layer of buttered greaseproof/waxed paper. Pour 1 pt/550 ml/2$\frac{1}{2}$ cups water into the pressure cooker. Position the trivet and stand the basin on top. Bring to pressure and cook for given time. Reduce pressure. Brown under a hot grill/broiler to serve.

COOKING TIME High/15-lb pressure 6 minutes
Reduce pressure slowly

SERVES 4

SOMERSET PEARS

INGREDIENTS	IMPERIAL	METRIC	AMERICAN
Medium pears, peeled, halved	4	4	4
Caster/superfine sugar	2 tbsp	2 tbsp	2 tbsp
Cider	$\frac{1}{4}$ pt	150 ml	$\frac{2}{3}$ cup
Water	$\frac{1}{4}$ pt	150 ml	$\frac{2}{3}$ cup
Juice 1 orange			
Apple jelly	2 tbsp	2 tbsp	2 tbsp
Cloves	2	2	2

Place the pear halves in the pressure cooker without the trivet and sprinkle the sugar over the pears. Add remaining ingredients, bring to pressure and cook for given time. Reduce pressure. Arrange the pears and liquor in a serving dish and chill them. Serve with ice cream.

COOKING TIME High/15-lb pressure 4–8 minutes
Reduce pressure quickly

SERVES 4

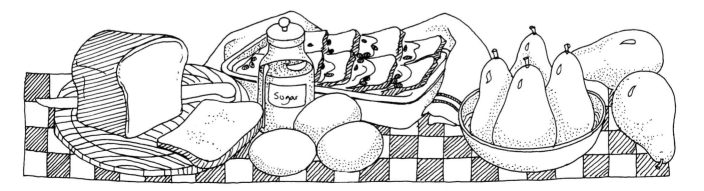

Lemon Apricots

Ingredients	Imperial	Metric	American
Dried apricots	12 oz	350 g	$\frac{3}{4}$ lb
Soft brown sugar	2 oz	50 g	$\frac{1}{4}$ cup
Grated rind and juice 1 lemon			
Sherry (optional)	2 tbsp	2 tbsp	2 tbsp
Flaked almonds	1 oz	25 g	3 tbsp

Place the apricots in a bowl and cover them with boiling water. Cover with a plate and leave for 1 hour. Drain the apricots, reserving the liquid, then arrange them in the pressure cooker without the trivet. Sprinkle the sugar, lemon rind, lemon juice and sherry over them. Make up the soaking liquid from the apricots to $\frac{3}{4}$ pt/400 ml/ 2 cups with water and pour it over the apricots. Bring to pressure and cook for given time. Reduce pressure. Serve hot or cold, scattered with flaked almonds.

Cooking Time High/15-lb pressure 3 minutes
Reduce pressure slowly

SERVES 6

Steamed Puddings

An ovenproof container should be used for puddings. Make sure it fits easily into the pressure cooker. When using ovenproof glass or china, it is advisable to add 5–10 minutes to the cooking time.

The container should not be more than two-thirds full – the pudding must have space to rise. It is a good idea, when covering the pudding, to make a pleat in the foil or greaseproof/waxed paper in case the pudding rises above the rim. Always secure the foil or greaseproof paper firmly on to the container, preferably with string.

Refer to your manufacturers' instructions about the amount of water to include for steaming. The quantity will depend on the cooking time but should not be less than $1\frac{1}{2}$ pt/1 1/4 cups.

A little vinegar in the water will prevent discoloration of the pressure cooker where hard water is used.

Take care not to allow the water to boil while preparing the pudding or you may not have sufficient water left for cooking. For the same reason it is a good idea to put boiling water into the pressure cooker rather than to bring cold water to the boil.

The trivet is used as a stand for the pudding.

Puddings are usually pre-steamed before pressure cooking. This helps to produce a light texture in the finished pudding. The lid is fitted on and the pressure cooker placed on a low heat (*without* the pressure weight or rotating valve) so that the water simmers and steam escapes gently from the vent. At the end of the pre-steaming period, the pressure weight or rotating valve is placed in position and the pressure cooker is brought to pressure for the required time.

Pressure should be reduced slowly.

When converting your own recipes for pressure-cooking the following guide may be useful:

Normal steaming time	Pre-steaming time	Pressure-cooking time Low/5-lb
30 minutes	5 minutes	10 minutes
1 hour	15 minutes	25 minutes
2–3 hours	20 minutes	50–60 minutes

PRESERVES AND BOTTLING

If you are a lover of home-made preserves, your pressure cooker will be a great time-saver. Marmalades, jams, jellies and chutneys can all be prepared in the pressure cooker.

Fruit for marmalades, jams and jellies is softened under pressure. When the sugar is added, the pressure cooker is used like an ordinary saucepan, without the lid, until the preserve reaches setting point.

Chutney ingredients are cooked under pressure, then reduced and thickened in the open pressure cooker for potting.

Bottling fruit is a simple and attractive way of preserving fresh, ripe summer produce. Nothing gives the cook or the family more pleasure than being able to eat juicy fruits in the middle of winter. Fruit bottling is considerably speeded up if you use your pressure cooker.

APPLE CHUTNEY

INGREDIENTS	IMPERIAL	METRIC	AMERICAN
Cooking apples, peeled, cored and diced	2 lb	1 kg	2 lb
Onions, chopped	2 lb	1 kg	2 lb
Sultanas/white raisins	4 oz	100 g	$\frac{2}{3}$ cup
Malt vinegar	$\frac{1}{2}$ pt	300 ml	$1\frac{1}{4}$ cups
Grated rind and juice of 1 lemon			
Ground cloves	1 tsp	1 tsp	1 tsp
Ground cinnamon	1 tsp	1 tsp	1 tsp
Ground ginger	1 tsp	1 tsp	1 tsp
Salt	1 tsp	1 tsp	1 tsp
Demerara/brown sugar	12 oz	350 g	$\frac{3}{4}$ lb

Place the apples, onions and sultanas in the pressure cooker with the vinegar, without the trivet. Bring to pressure and cook for given time. Reduce pressure. Add the remaining ingredients and heat them gently until the sugar dissolves. Bring to the boil and simmer in the open pressure cooker until the chutney thickens. Pour into warmed, dry jars. Cover and label.

COOKING TIME High/15-lb pressure 12 minutes
Reduce pressure slowly

MAKES ABOUT 4 lb/1.8 kg

RHUBARB CHUTNEY

INGREDIENTS	IMPERIAL	METRIC	AMERICAN
Rhubarb, sliced	3 lb	1.4 kg	3 lb
Onions, chopped	8 oz	225 g	$\frac{1}{2}$ lb
Ground ginger	1 tsp	1 tsp	1 tsp
Mixed spice	2 tsp	2 tsp	2 tsp
Salt	1 tsp	1 tsp	1 tsp
Malt vinegar	$\frac{3}{4}$ pt	400 ml	2 cups
Sugar	1 lb	450 g	1 lb

Place all the ingredients, except the sugar, in the pressure cooker, without the trivet. Bring to pressure and cook for given time. Reduce pressure.

Add the sugar and heat gently until it dissolves. Bring to the boil and simmer gently in the open pressure cooker until the chutney thickens. Pour into warmed, dry jars. Cover and label.

COOKING TIME High/15-lb pressure 4 minutes
Reduce pressure slowly

MAKES 3 lb/1.4 kg

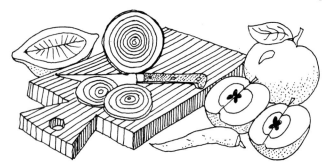

GREEN TOMATO CHUTNEY

INGREDIENTS	IMPERIAL	METRIC	AMERICAN
Green tomatoes, thinly sliced	3 lb	1.4 kg	3 lb
Onions, chopped	8 oz	225 g	$\frac{1}{2}$ lb
Cooking apples, peeled, cored and chopped	1 lb	450 g	1 lb
Sultanas/white raisins	8 oz	225 g	$1\frac{1}{3}$ cups
Salt	2 tbsp	2 tbsp	2 tbsp
Malt vinegar	$\frac{3}{4}$ pt	400 ml	2 cups
Dry mustard	1 tsp	1 tsp	1 tsp
Ground ginger	1 tsp	1 tsp	1 tsp
Cayenne pepper	$\frac{1}{2}$ tsp	$\frac{1}{2}$ tsp	$\frac{1}{2}$ tsp
Demerara/brown sugar	8 oz	225 g	$\frac{1}{2}$ lb

Place all the ingredients, except the sugar, in the pressure cooker without the trivet. Bring to pressure and cook for given time. Reduce pressure.

Add the sugar and heat gently until it dissolves. Bring to the boil and simmer gently in the open pressure cooker until the chutney thickens. Pour into warmed, dry jars. Cover and label.

COOKING TIME High/15-lb pressure 10 minutes
Reduce pressure slowly

MAKES ABOUT 3 lb/1.4 kg

LEMON CURD

INGREDIENTS	IMPERIAL	METRIC	AMERICAN
Eggs, beaten	4	4	4
Sugar	1 lb	450 g	1 lb
Finely grated rind of 4 lemons			
Lemons, strained juice	2	2	2
Unsalted butter, cut into small pieces	4 oz	100 g	$\frac{1}{2}$ cup

Strain the beaten eggs into an ovenproof basin and stir in the sugar, lemon rind, lemon juice and butter pieces. Securely tie on a double layer of buttered greaseproof/waxed paper. Pour $\frac{1}{2}$ pt/300 ml/$1\frac{1}{4}$ cups water into the pressure cooker and position the trivet. Stand the basin on the trivet, bring to pressure and cook for given time. Reduce pressure. Stir the lemon curd and pour into warmed, dry jars. Cool, cover and label.

COOKING TIME High/15-lb pressure 10 minutes
Reduce pressure slowly

NOTE Lemon Curd may be stored for up to 2 months only.

MAKES ABOUT 2 lb/1 kg

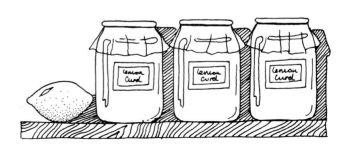

TANGERINE AND GINGER CURD

INGREDIENTS	IMPERIAL	METRIC	AMERICAN
Finely grated rind and juice of 3 tangerines			
Lemon juice	1 tbsp	1 tbsp	1 tbsp
Egg yolks	3	3	3
Caster/superfine sugar	4½ oz	115 g	generous ½ cup
Unsalted butter, diced	4 oz	100 g	½ cup
Finely chopped preserved ginger	3 tbsp	3 tbsp	3 tbsp

Grate the rind from two of the tangerines. Squeeze the juice from all of them. Strain the tangerine and lemon juice into an ovenproof dish or bowl that will fit easily inside the cooker. Strain in the egg yolks, then stir in the sugar and butter. Cover with a double thickness of greaseproof/waxed paper and tie in place. Pour 300 ml/½ pint/1¼ cups water into the pressure cooker. Position the trivet. Stand the bowl on the trivet, bring to pressure and cook for given time. Reduce pressure.

Stir the ginger into the curd and pour into warmed, dry jars. Cool, cover and label.

COOKING TIME Medium/10-lb pressure 10 minutes
Reduce pressure slowly

NOTE The curd may be stored for up to 2 months only and should be kept in a cool, dark place.

MAKES 1 lb/450 g

ORANGE MARMALADE

INGREDIENTS	IMPERIAL	METRIC	AMERICAN
Seville oranges	1½ lb	700 g	1½ lb
Water	1 pt	550 ml	2½ cups
Juice 1 lemon			
Sugar	3 lb	1.4 kg	3 lb

Remove the peel from the oranges, using a sharp knife or potato peeler and making sure no pith is attached. Cut the peel into pieces. Cut the oranges in half and squeeze out the juice. Tie the pith and pips in a piece of muslin/cheesecloth and soak in the water overnight. Place the water, muslin bag, peel and lemon juice in the pressure cooker. Bring to pressure and cook for given time. Reduce pressure.

Cool the liquid sufficiently to squeeze the juice from the muslin bag into the orange liquor. Stir in the sugar. Discard the muslin bag. Heat the marmalade gently until the sugar dissolves, then boil it rapidly in the open pressure cooker until setting point is reached (see page 107). To prevent the peel rising in the jars, cool the marmalade until a skin begins to form on top (about 15 minutes), then pour it into warmed, dry jars and cover with wax discs. Cool, cover and label.

COOKING TIME High/15-lb pressure 10–15 minutes
Reduce pressure slowly

NOTE Marmalade may also be prepared by the quick method detailed for Ginger Marmalade. Photograph on page 2.

MAKES 4–5 lb/1.8–2.3 kg

GRAPEFRUIT AND WHISKY MARMALADE

INGREDIENTS	IMPERIAL	METRIC	AMERICAN
Grapefruit (about 3)	2 lb	1 kg	2 lb
Pips, grated rind and juice of 2 lemons			
Water	$1\frac{1}{2}$ pt	900 ml	$3\frac{3}{4}$ cups
Preserving or granulated sugar, warmed	4 lb	2 kg	4 lb
Scotch whisky	3 fl oz	75 ml	6 tbsp

Wash the grapefruit, remove the rind using a sharp knife and cut it into thin strips. Remove the pith and pips from the grapefruit flesh and tie in muslin/cheesecloth bag with the lemon pips. Place the muslin bag in the cooker with the grapefruit rind and flesh and lemon rind and juice. Add the water, bring to pressure and cook for given time. Reduce pressure.

Remove the muslin bag and allow to cool slightly. Squeeze the bag over the cooked fruit to collect as much juice and pectin as possible, then discard.

Return the open pressure cooker to a low heat, add the warmed sugar and stir, using a wooden spoon, until the sugar has dissolved. Boil rapidly until setting point is reached. Remove from the heat, remove any scum using a slotted spoon, then stir in the whisky. Skim and allow to stand for 10–15 minutes, then stir to distribute the peel. Ladle into warmed, dry jars. Cover and label.

COOKING TIME Medium/10-lb pressure 10–12 minutes
Reduce pressure slowly

MAKES ABOUT 6 lb/2.7 kg

GINGER MARMALADE

INGREDIENTS	IMPERIAL	METRIC	AMERICAN
Seville oranges	3	3	3
Water	1 pt	550 ml	$2\frac{1}{2}$ cups
Cooking apples, peeled, cored and grated	$1\frac{1}{2}$ lb	700 g	$1\frac{1}{2}$ lb
Sugar	3 lb	1.4 kg	3 lb
Preserved ginger, chopped	4 oz	100 g	$\frac{1}{4}$ lb
Ground ginger	2 tsp	2 tsp	2 tsp

Wash the oranges and place them whole in the pressure cooker with the water, without the trivet. Bring to pressure and cook for given time. Reduce pressure.

Cool sufficiently to cut the peel (but no pith) off the oranges and chop it. Cut the oranges in half, squeeze out the juice and strain it.

Add this, with the orange peel, to the liquor. Tie the pips in a muslin/cheesecloth bag and add them to the pressure cooker with the apples. Boil the marmalade for 5 minutes, then remove the muslin bag and discard it. Add the sugar and heat gently until dissolved. Stir in the preserved and ground ginger. Boil rapidly until setting point is reached (see page 107).

To prevent the peel rising in the jars, cool the marmalade until a skin begins to form on top (about 15 minutes), then pour it into warmed, dry jars and cover with wax discs. Cool, cover and label.

COOKING TIME High/15-lb pressure 10–15 minutes
Reduce pressure slowly

MAKES ABOUT 5 lb/2.3 kg

ALMOND APRICOT JAM

INGREDIENTS	IMPERIAL	METRIC	AMERICAN
Dried apricots, washed and cup up	1 lb	450 g	1 lb
Boiling water	2 pt	1 l	5 cups
Juice 1 lemon			
Sugar	3 lb	1.4 kg	3 lb
Blanched almonds	2 oz	50 g	$\frac{1}{3}$ cup

Put the apricots in the pressure cooker with the boiling water, without the trivet. Cover and leave for 1 hour. Add the lemon juice, bring to pressure and cook for given time. Reduce pressure.

Add the sugar and heat gently until it dissolves. Stir in the almonds and boil the jam rapidly in the open pressure cooker until setting point is reached (see page 107). Pour the jam into warmed, dry jars and cover with waxed discs. Cool, cover and label.

COOKING TIME High/15-lb pressure 10 minutes
Reduce pressure slowly

MAKES 4–5 lb/1.8–2.3 kg

DAMSON AND PORT JAM

INGREDIENTS	IMPERIAL	METRIC	AMERICAN
Damsons	3 lb	1.4 kg	3 lb
Water	$\frac{1}{2}$ pt	300 ml	$1\frac{1}{4}$ cups
Preserving sugar, warmed	3 lb	1.4 kg	3 lb
Port	4 tbsp	4 tbsp	4 tbsp
Knob of butter			

Wash and dry the fruit and prick each damson 2–3 times with a knitting needle. Put the fruit and water into the pressure cooker. Bring to pressure and cook for given time. Reduce pressure.

Add the sugar to the open cooker and stir over a low heat until the sugar has completely dissolved. Boil rapidly until setting point is reached, about 20 minutes. Remove from the heat and stir in the port and a small knob of butter. Remove the stones using a slotted spoon. Pour the jam into warmed, dry jars. Cover and label.

COOKING TIME Medium/10-lb pressure 8 minutes
Reduce pressure slowly

MAKES ABOUT 5 lb/2.3 kg

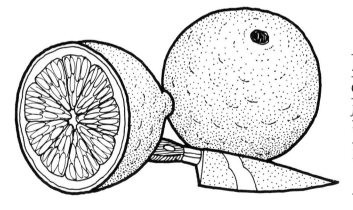

APPLE JELLY

INGREDIENTS	IMPERIAL	METRIC	AMERICAN
Cooking apples	3 lb	1.4 kg	3 lb
Juice 1 lemon			
Water	1 pt	550 ml	$2\frac{1}{2}$ cups
Proportion of sugar to strained juice 1 lb/450 g per	1 pt	550 ml	$2\frac{1}{2}$ cups

Wash the apples, removing any bruised parts, and cut them into thick slices (but do not peel or core them). Place the apples in the pressure cooker with the lemon juice and water, without the trivet. Bring to pressure and cook for given time. Reduce pressure.

Mash the apples and strain them through a jelly bag or double layer of cloth (such as a tea towel or sheeting). Measure the strained juice and put it back into the pressure cooker with the correct amount of sugar. Heat gently until the sugar dissolves, then boil rapidly in the open pressure cooker until setting point is reached (see page 107). Pour the jelly into warmed, dry jars and cover with wax discs. Cool, cover and label.

COOKING TIME High/15-lb pressure 3 minutes
Reduce pressure slowly

CHECKPOINT If the juice is allowed to drip through the jelly bag or cloth, the result will be clearer than if it is forced through.

REDCURRANT JELLY

As for apple jelly, using 3 lb/1.4 kg redcurrants with $\frac{1}{2}$ pt/300 ml/1$\frac{1}{4}$ cups water. To each 1 pt/550 ml/2$\frac{1}{2}$ cups strained juice add 1$\frac{1}{4}$ lb/550 g sugar.

BLACKCURRANT JELLY

As for apple jelly, using 3 lb/1.4 kg blackcurrants with 1$\frac{3}{4}$ pt/1 1/4$\frac{1}{2}$ cups water. To each 1 pt/550 ml/2$\frac{1}{2}$ cups strained juice add 1 lb/450 g sugar.

MARMALADES, JAMS AND JELLIES

When softening fruit under pressure, fill the pressure cooker no more than half full.

The trivet is not used.

Choose fresh, ripe, firm, unblemished fruit for a good result.

Softening the fruit helps to release the pectin (the setting agent) in fruit. Some fruits contain more than others, and you may need to mix fruits or to add lemon to compensate.

High-pectin fruits: damsons, blackcurrants, redcurrants, gooseberries.

Medium-pectin fruits: apricots, greengages, loganberries, plums, raspberries.

Low-pectin fruits: blackberries, cherries, marrow, pears, rhubarb, strawberries.

Warmed sugar will take less time to dissolve and will produce a preserve of better colour and flavour.

Once the sugar has been added the lid *must not* be replaced on the pressure cooker. Use the pressure cooker base as an ordinary pan.

There are three methods of checking that the jam has reached setting point:
1. The temperature test is the most accurate method. The jam will set when it reaches a temperature of 221°F (104°C).
2. Place a little of the jam on to a cold plate. When the jam is cool, push your finger across its surface. If it wrinkles, you must have a set. During this test remember to move the pressure cooker off the heat to avoid boiling the jam too long.
3. Stir the jam with a wooden spoon and lift it out. The jam will begin to set on the spoon when setting point is reached.

When adapting your own recipes for pressure-cooking, reduce the liquid by about half (but make sure you include the minimum amount recommended in your instruction book). Generally, allow 1 lb/450 g sugar per 1 lb/450 g fruit.

BOTTLING

CHECKPOINTS FOR BOTTLING FRUIT The trivet should be used for bottling.

Remember to add to the pressure cooker at least the minimum amount of water recommended by your manufacturer. Check the instruction book for your particular pressure cooker.

Choose bottles which will fit easily into the pressure cooker. When stood on the trivet, they should not touch each other or the sides or lid of the pressure cooker.

Make sure the bottling jars are not damaged in any way. The rubber rings must be flexible and fit the neck of the jar snugly.

Fruits should be ripe, firm and unblemished. Choose fruits of similar size and ripeness.

Fruit can be bottled in water, but a better result is obtained if a syrup is used. To make syrup:

Light syrup: suitable for fruit to be used for tarts, crumbles etc. Boil 2–4 oz/50–100 g/4–8 tbsp sugar in each 1 pt/550 ml/2½ cups water.

Heavy syrup: suitable for fruit to be used straight as a dessert or for soft fruits which are liable to float in the jar. Boil 6–8 oz/175–225 g/¾–1 cup sugar in each 1 pt/ 550 ml/2½ cups water.

TO BOTTLE FRUIT Wash and rinse the jars and lids. Stand them in boiling water till ready to use.

Wash the fruit and prepare according to kind. Pack it firmly into the jars to the shoulder.

Pour boiling syrup over the fruit, leaving ¼ inch/0.5 cm headspace. To eliminate air bubbles, pour in a little syrup at a time, tapping the jar gently after each addition.

Fit rubber band and tops on the jars. With metal screw bands, screw on till tight, then unscrew turn. Jars with metal clips should be sealed.

Place the trivet in the pressure cooker with boiling water (check with instruction book for correct amount, usually about 2 pt/1.1 l/5 cups. Stand the jars on the trivet.

Bring to pressure on medium heat and cook for given time (see chart following). Reduce pressure slowly.

Fruit	Cooking time at Medium/10-lb pressure
Apples, quarters, thick slices	1 minute
Apricots, whole	1 minute
Blackberries	1 minute
Blackcurrants, Redcurrants	1 minute
Cherries, whole	1 minute
Damsons, Greengages, Plums, whole	1 minute
Gooseberries	1 minute
Peaches, skinned halves	3 minutes
Pears, peeled, cored and halved	3 minutes
Raspberries	1 minute
Rhubarb	1 minute
Strawberries	3 minutes
Tomatoes, skinned, whole	3 minutes

PRESSURE COOKING TIME CHARTS

MEAT

The following times for pressure-cooking joints are for High/15-lb pressure.

	Cooking time per lb/450 g at High/15-lb pressure
Beef	
Rolled sirloin or rump	10 minutes
Topside, rolled rump	12 minutes
Silverside	15 minutes
Lamb	
Breast, boned and rolled	12 minutes
Leg	15 minutes
Pork	
Fillet	12 minutes
Shoulder or loin, boned and rolled	15 minutes
Veal	
Knuckle	10 minutes
Fillet, loin	12 minutes
Shoulder, boned or breast, boned and rolled	14 minutes
Bacon	12 minutes
Ox tongue	15 minutes

POULTRY AND GAME

The following times for pressure-cooking poultry and game are for High/15-lb pressure.

Poultry and Game		Cooking time at High/15-lb pressure
Chicken:		
Poussin,	halved	7 minutes
	joints	4 minutes
Roasting,	whole	5 minutes per 1 lb/450 g
	joints	5–7 minutes (depending on size)
Boiling,	whole	10 minutes per 1 lb/450 g
	joints	10–15 minutes (depending on size)
Turkey,	joints	10 minutes
Duck,	whole	12–15 minutes per 1 lb/450 g
	joints	12 minutes
Grouse		10 minutes
Pigeons		10 minutes
Hare,	joints	40 minutes
Rabbit,	joints	15 minutes
Pheasant, Partridge	whole	7–10 minutes (depending on age)
	joints	5–7 minutes (depending on age)

FISH

The following times for pressure-cooking fish are for High/15-lb pressure.

White fish	*Cooking time at High/15-lb pressure*
Bass, Bream, Brill, Cod, Coley, Haddock, Hake, Halibut, Ling, Plaice, Rock Salmon, Sole, Turbot	Steaks and fillets 3–6 minutes Whole fish 5–6 minutes per 1 lb/450 g
Skate wings	3–6 minutes
Whiting	Steaks and fillets 4–5 minutes Whole fish 5–6 minutes per 1 lb/450 g
Oily fish	
Herring, Mackerel, Mullet, Trout	Whole fish 5–8 minutes
Salmon	Steaks 6–8 minutes Whole fish 6 minutes per 1 lb/450 g
Shellfish	
Crab	7–10 minutes
Lobster	10 minutes
Prawns, Shrimps	2–3minutes

VEGETABLES

The following times for pressure-cooking fresh vegetables are for High/15-lb pressure. Blanching times are for Medium/10-lb pressure only.

Vegetable	Cooking time High/15-lb pressure	Blanching time Medium/10-lb pressure
Artichokes, Globe	6–10 minutes depending on size	3–5 minutes depending on size
Jerusalem	4–6 minutes	
Asparagus, bundles	2–4 minutes	bring to pressure only
Beans, Broad	3–5 minutes	1 minute
French	3 minutes	bring to pressure only
Runner	4 minutes	bring to pressure only
Beetroot/Beet, small	10 minutes	7 minutes, sliced
medium	15–20 minutes	
large	20–30 minutes	
Broccoli spears	3–4 minutes	1 minute
Brussels Sprouts	3–4 minutes	1 minute
Cabbage, shredded	3 minutes	bring to pressure only
Carrots, sliced	3–4 minutes	2 minutes
Cauliflower, florets	3–4 minutes	1 minute
whole	5–8 minutes	
Celery, short sticks	3 minutes	2 minutes
Celeriac, cubes	3 minutes	1 minute
Chicory, whole	3–6 minutes	
Corn on the cob	3–5 minutes depending on size	2–3 minutes depending on size
Courgettes/zucchini, sliced	3 minutes	bring to pressure only
Fennel, halves	3–6 minutes	1 minute
Leeks, sliced	3–4 minutes	1 minute
Marrow, thick slices	3–4 minutes	2 minutes
Onions, whole	6–8 minutes	
sliced	3–4 minutes	
Parsnips, sliced	3–4 minutes	1 minute
Peas	3–4 minutes	1 minute
Potatoes, new whole	4–5 minutes	2 minutes
old quarters	3–4 minutes	
Spinach	1–2 minutes	bring to pressure only
Swede, cubes	4 minutes	1 minute
Turnip, sliced or small whole	3–4 minutes	2 minutes

DRIED VEGETABLES

Dried vegetables do not need overnight soaking. Put the vegetables into a large bowl and cover them with plenty of boiling water. Put a plate over the bowl and leave the beans to soak for one hour.

Pour into the pressure cooker $1\frac{3}{4}$ pt/1 l/$4\frac{1}{2}$ cups liquid for every 1 lb/450 g vegetables. Make up the soaking water from the vegetables to the required amount with more water.

Bring to the boil and add the vegetables. The pressure cooker should not be more than half full. Season to taste and bring it back to the boil.

Skim the surface of the liquid, then lower the heat till the contents boil gently. Bring to pressure on this heat and cook for the given time.

Always reduce pressure slowly.

Dried vegetable	Cooking time at High/15-lb pressure
Butter/lima beans	20 minutes
Haricot/navy beans, small	20 minutes
large	30 minutes
Lentils	15 minutes
Peas, whole	20 minutes
split	15 minutes

NOTE Split varieties, such as lentils or peas, may be added to soups, casseroles etc., without pre-soaking.

FRESH FRUIT

Fruit	Cooking time at High/15-lb pressure
Apricots, Cherries, Damsons, Greengages (halved) Pears, Peaches (halved)	Bring to pressure 3–5 minutes
Hard pears	8–10 minutes

	Medium/10-lb pressure
Blackcurrants, Gooseberries, Loganberries, Raspberries, Plums, Rhubarb	Bring to pressure only on medium heat
Apple (slices)	1 minute

DRIED FRUIT

Place the fruit in a bowl and cover it with boiling water. Pour over 1 pt/550 ml/$2\frac{1}{2}$ cups for every 1 lb/450 g dried fruit. Cover with a plate and leave to stand for 10 minutes.

Place the fruit and soaking liquid in the pressure cooker (without the trivet) and add sugar and flavourings (such as lemon or orange rind and juice, cloves, spices) to taste.

Do not fill the pressure cooker more than half full, as the fruit will expand during cooking.

Bring to pressure and cook for given time (see table below). Reduce pressure slowly.

Fruit	Cooking time at High/15-lb pressure
Apples	6 minutes
Apricots	3 minutes
Figs, Pears, Prunes, Mixed Fruit	10 minutes
Peaches	5 minutes

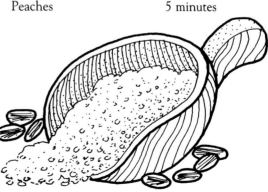

HOW TO USE YOUR PRESSURE COOKER

It is essential to follow the manufacturers' instructions for your particular model very carefully to obtain good results. When giving general instructions for use below, I have separated the main sorts of pressure cookers into types.

Type 1 has a Speedset pressure control.

Type 2 has a pressure weight with an indicator plunger (Weight A, diagram p. 113).

Type 3 has a pressure weight consisting of fitted rings (Weight B, diagram p. 115).

Type 4 has a fixed $7\frac{1}{2}$-lb pressure (diagram p. 116).

TYPES 1, 2 AND 3

1. Put the prepared food into the pressure cooker along with the accurate amount of liquid. Usually the minimum amount needed is $\frac{1}{2}$ pt/300 ml/$1\frac{1}{4}$ cups, but check the manufacturers' instructions to make sure. The quantity required will depend on the recipe being followed and the length of cooking time. The liquid used must always be one which gives off steam when it boils, e.g. water, stock, fruit juice, cider, wine.

Remember to leave sufficient space above the food for steam to circulate or for foods to rise in the pressure cooker.

2. Place the lid in position, ensuring that it is firmly locked.

3. Place the pressure cooker on the heat.

TYPE 1 (Photograph on page 6)

4. Clip the Speedset pressure control on to the steam vent. The lever must be switched so it is pointing to the '0' on the housing.

5. As the temperature inside the cooker increases the air will be expelled and the automatic air vent (under the housing) will seal.

6. Once the pressure begins to increase the visual indicator inside the Speedset pressure control will begin to rise. The indicator consists of three coloured bands to correspond with the pressure given in the recipes:

Yellow band	Low/5-lb pressure
Blue band	Medium/10-lb pressure
Red band	High/15-lb pressure

Once the desired colour band is *just* showing the pressure required, reduce the heat to maintain this pressure.

TYPE 2

4. Place the indicator weight firmly in position on the central vent and turn the heat up full.

5. As the liquid boils, the pressure cooker fills with steam, some of which will be seen coming through the automatic air vent. This air vent will seal itself automatically, then the indicator plunger will rise as the pressure rises.

6. When the required pressure has been reached, shown by the number of silver rings (or coloured bands as on Type 1), turn the heat down to maintain this pressure.

Time the cooking from now.

TYPE 3

4. Place the correct weight firmly in position on the central vent. Turn the heat up full.

5. As the liquid boils, the pressure cooker fills with steam, expelling all the air. When the pressure builds up sufficiently inside the pressure cooker a slight hissing sound will be heard, followed by a much louder one as steam begins to escape. Do not leave the pressure cooker during this stage.

6. A continuous loud hissing indicates that pressure has now been reached, so turn down the heat until a continuous gentle 'muttering' is heard. This should be maintained throughout the cooking time.

Time the cooking from now.

TYPES 1, 2 AND 3

7. At the end of the cooking time, remove the pressure cooker from the heat. Pressure must be reduced before removing the pressure weight or the lid. There are two methods of doing this.

a. *Slow method*

This slower method should be used when:

cooking liquid foods (such as soups and stews) and dried vegetables, all of which are liable to spurt out of the vent pipe on sudden reduction of pressure.

cooking egg custards and milk puddings which would curdle or separate with a sudden temperature drop, cooking puddings containing a raising agent, which would sink with a sudden temperature drop, and bottling, where a sudden temperature drop would cause the jars to crack.

Type 2

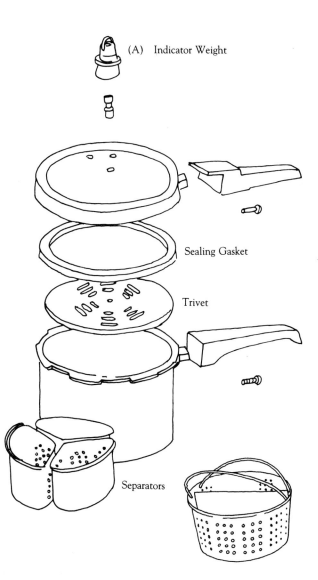

(A) Indicator Weight

Sealing Gasket

Trivet

Separators

113

Type 3

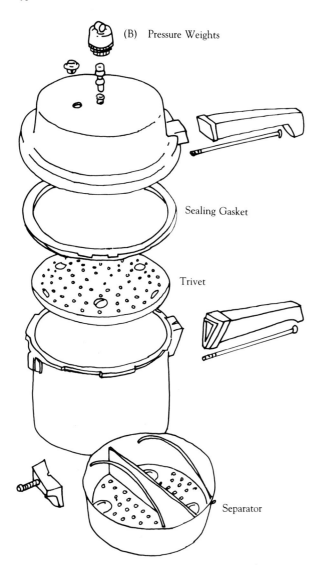

(B) Pressure Weights

Sealing Gasket

Trivet

Separator

Types 1 and 2

Reduce pressure slowly by allowing the pressure cooker to stand at room temperature, away from the heat, until the indicator plunger has dropped so no silver rings or coloured bands are visible, and the metal plunger if there is one in the automatic air vent has dropped to its normal position. The weight if there is one can now be lifted off and the lid removed.

Type 3

Reduce pressure slowly by allowing the pressure cooker to stand at room temperature, away from the heat. To test whether pressure has been reduced, lift the weight slightly. When no more steam escapes the weight can be lifted off and the lid removed.

b. *Quick method*
Type 1

Reduce pressure quickly by turning the pressure release lever to the left to the 'steam' position. Steam and pressure will be released through the steam housing.

Types 2 and 3

Reduce pressure with cold water by standing the pressure cooker in a bowl of cold water.

This method should be used when the cooking time is vital. For example, vegetables would overcook if pressure was not reduced this way.

Note Each recipe in this book indicates the correct method for reducing pressure.

Type 4

1. Put the prepared food into the pressure cooker with the correct amount of liquid (refer to the manufacturers' instructions on the minimum quantity needed for particular recipes or methods of cooking). Remember that the liquid used must be one which gives off steam when it boils and do leave sufficient space above the food for steam to circulate or for foods to rise.
2. Place the lid in position by sliding it on horizontally and fitting it carefully on to the rim of the pan. To tighten the lid, turn the knob in the direction of the arrow through two complete turns. The lid is now tight and locked.
3. Position the rotating valve by placing it vertically on the vent on the lid and push down as far as it will go.

4. Place the pressure cooker on the heat. As pressure is reached the valve begins to turn, emitting steam. *Time cooking from now.* Reduce the heat so that the valve remains still most of the time. A little steam will still be released, and the valve will occasionally turn slowly.

5. At the end of the cooking time, remove the pressure cooker from the heat. Lower the pressure by lifting the rotating valve up to the first notch (do not remove it completely). This allows the steam to escape while the pressure falls. When all the steam has been expelled the lid can be removed. Do this by turning the knob in the opposite direction to the arrow until the clamp touches the lid. Lift the lid and slide it out horizontally.

If pressure is not reduced as soon as cooking is completed, the cooling steam condenses inside the pressure cooker, forming a vacuum and thus holding down the lid. If this should happen, reheat the pressure cooker for a few seconds with the knob in the open position. The lid will loosen itself.

NOTE Since more steam is lost during cooking with pressure cooker Type 4, more liquid is needed. Cooking times will be longer than those for Types 1, 2 and 3 as the cooking pressure is lower.

SAFETY

All pressure cookers include safety devices which operate if the vent pipe becomes blocked or if the pressure cooker boils dry and over-heats. Should the safety devices come into operation, the excess pressure is automatically released from the pressure cooker. However, if the manufacturers' instructions are carefully followed, the safety devices should never need to activate.

As a general rule, never fill the pressure cooker more than two-thirds full with solids or half-full with liquids or other foods that tend to boil over (for example, soups, milk, cereals, pastas). Sufficient space must always be left above the food for steam to circulate and for foods to rise.

Type 4

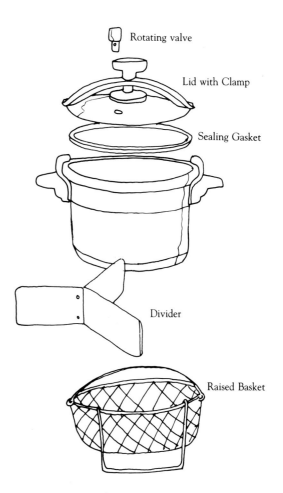

Rotating valve

Lid with Clamp

Sealing Gasket

Divider

Raised Basket

WEIGHTS AND MEASURES

Ingredients used in the recipes are given in Imperial, Metric and American measures. Generally speaking, the metric and American measures are not exact equivalents of their imperial counterparts. I find it better to work in quantities which have been rounded off to convenient measures. Where I have felt it important to be accurate, exact equivalents are given. It is wise to follow one set of measures throughout a recipe; do not skip from one set to another.

All spoon and cup measures are level unless otherwise stated.

The imperial pint measures 20 fl oz; the American pint measures 16 fl oz.

When cans of food are included in a recipe, the weights given on the label are quoted – these are usually exact equivalents.

When converting your own recipes from imperial to metric quantities, or vice versa, use the following tables as guidelines.

CAPACITY

Imperial	Metric
$\frac{1}{4}$ pt (5 fl oz)	150 ml
$\frac{1}{2}$ pt (10 fl oz)	300 ml
$\frac{3}{4}$ pt (15 fl oz)	400 ml
1 pt (20 fl oz)	500–600 ml
$1\frac{1}{2}$ pt	900 ml
$1\frac{3}{4}$ pt	1 l
2 pt	1.1 l

WEIGHT

Imperial	Metric
1 oz	25 g
2 oz	50 g
3 oz	75 g
4 oz	100–125 g
5 oz	150 g
6 oz	175 g
8 oz	225 g
10 oz	275 g
12 oz	350 g
14 oz	400 g
16 oz (1 lb)	450 g
$1\frac{1}{2}$ lb	700 g
2 lb	900 g
3 lb	1.4 kg

QUANTITIES

Most of the recipes in this book are for four people. Some are for six or occasionally more.

These quantities may be halved or quartered as long as the minimum amount of liquid recommended in your instruction book is included. Remember that the amount of liquid used depends on the cooking time and on the size of your pressure cooker, and *not* on the amount of food being cooked.

When doubling up on quantities, check the appropriate section of the book to see how full the pressure cooker should be.

INDEX